Creating & Crafting
the Contemporary English Version

⁊

A New Approach
to Bible Translation

Creating & Crafting

the Contemporary English Version

A New Approach
to Bible Translation

by

Barclay M. Newman
Senior Translations Officer,
ABS Translations Department

and

Charles S. Houser
Erroll F. Rhodes
David G. Burke
Editors, ABS Translations Department

AMERICAN BIBLE SOCIETY
NEW YORK

Creating & Crafting
the Contemporary English Version

Printed in the United States of America
Creating & Crafting the CEV-105662
ABS-12/96-2,900-4,600-B2

ISBN 0-8267-0033-

FOREWORD

It has been a privilege as the President of the ABS to see the 175-year-old organization wrestle with the need for new generations to encounter the Word of God — and doing so in translations and formats that these people will find especially meaningful. It was especially exciting to witness the birth of a new Bible translation — the *Contemporary English Version.*

Work on the *CEV* began in 1984 when Dr. Barclay Newman, Ph.D., a distinguished biblical scholar who had provided several decades of service as a translations consultant in the Asia Pacific Region of the United Bible Societies, first began to apply his considerable knowledge to his own first language — English. He meticulously studied the language that people, and especially children, used and were exposed to on a daily basis through books, magazines, newspapers, the movies, and television. This eclectic and careful study helped him to understand what terms and sentence structures were most understandable to people who used English in their day to day communication. He learned what sorts of constructions confused readers, and even more significantly, he learned which terms and grammatical constructions were likely to be misunderstood by people who *heard* texts being read aloud.

All of this knowledge guided Dr. Newman as he developed translation principles for the *Contemporary English Version* and as he prepared the draft of the first "test" publication in this translation. That book, published in 1986, was a collection of Scripture passages on the life of Jesus and was published as an illustrated edition for children. Response to this initial publication was warm, as expected. Children loved it. Teachers and parents loved it, too — many confessing that they enjoyed it for themselves. People asked when further publications would be available in this same translation. "When will you have the whole Bible? This is something I can understand!"

Needless to say, preparing a translation of God's Holy Word is not something the American Bible Society was willing to dash off in a slap-dash manner. As with the translators of the *King James Version* Bible 375 years before them, the ABS needed time to assemble and train the right personnel for this project. And theological and linguistic experts needed time to review each draft the translation team prepared. In 1991, the 175th anniversary of the American Bible Society, the ABS published the full New Testament. Its acceptance by individuals and the churches was, again, enthusiastic. And it is exciting that four years later the Bible is at long last available in this easy to understand translation.

Rather than taking time and space to sing the praises of the *CEV*, I invite you to read this collection of essays. Each one explains a different aspect of what the translators have accomplished. Each one will give you new information about what goes into making a faithful translation of the Hebrew and Greek texts that are the basis of all good translations. And each one will show you how carefully the translators worked to make the *Contemporary English Version* a joy to read. An appendix at the back of the book will introduce you to Dr. Newman's partners in this historical endeavor. Another appendix will give you an opportunity to enjoy reading a few passages in this translation for yourself. Give yourself this treat. Take the time to enjoy the ringing clarity, beauty and wonder of God's Word.

Eugene B. Habecker
President
American Bible Society

PREFACE

This book is designed to give the reader a brief glimpse beyond the surface of the *Contemporary English Version* Bible. Because this translation is clear and easy for anyone with an understanding of English to follow, people who encounter this translation — whether reading a print edition for themselves or hearing it read aloud during congregational worship — may not realize the amount of careful thought and scholarly knowledge that went into the creating and crafting of the text.

The essays in this book address a number of topics relating to the development of this new translation. They may be read in sequence, by anyone wanting a good introduction into modern translation principles and processes and to the *CEV* specifically. Or, they may be read selectively or out of sequence by persons interested in specific aspects or features of the *CEV* — such as "What makes this translation so easy to understand?" (chapter 2), or "At what grade level is this text written?" (chapter 4), or "How does the *CEV* treat poetry?" (chapter 5).

Every church group and church member has questions about the many English translations now available to them. Which translation is best for children's Sunday school classes? Which is best for reading aloud during worship services? Which works well when trying to reach out to people who have never gone to church before — or, to people who have been to church but have always found it a struggle to understand traditional Bible translations and church language. Which translation is easiest to share with someone learning English as a second language. Choosing a Bible translation for a particular use may be a personal decision, or it may require the approval of an education committee or an entire church board. Many questions will surface, each one worthy of careful consideration. It is hoped that the essays in this book will aid understanding the process of Bible translation better, so that your decision will be the right one for the individuals or groups you want to reach with the Word of God.

Chapter 1, *Introduction: A Translation in the Spirit of the King James Version*, shows how the translators of the *Contemporary English Version* have taken many of their cues from the principles first set down by the translators of the *King James Version* Bible almost 400 years ago. Their reverence for the Scriptures, their commitment to faithfully communicating the meaning of the original language texts in English that people could understand, and their humility before the Holy Spirit as they undertook their task is something the *CEV* translators have emulated.

Chapter 2, *Facing the Problem: Millions of People Can Barely Read or Write*, offers many specific examples of how the translators challenged themselves to find clear, unambiguous ways of communicating the Scripture texts in English that are as natural-sounding as the English we hear spoken every day. Factors discussed include: avoidance of slang, attention to sentence length and rhythms, audience sensitivity, and the introduction of format features that help the reader understand difficult books of the Bible. Chapter 3, *Finding Solutions: Using Language People Can Understand*, continues the discussion of how the *CEV* addresses the need to provide an easy-to-follow translation. Discussion here centers on how specific important theological concepts are expressed while avoiding abstract terminology that the new Bible reader would have difficulty understanding.

A brief overview of what makes a written text readable is undertaken in chapter 4, *Finding a Place: How To Evaluate the Readability of a Bible Translation*. This chapter shows how evaluating the readability of a translation consists of more than just counting the number of letters in a word, the number of words in a sentence and the number of sentences in a paragraph. In this chapter, seven additional readability factors are identified and it is demonstrated how the translators of the *CEV* were able to implement these factors by attending to "small matters" that make a big difference.

The translators of the *CEV* have made a special effort to be sure that the poetic passages of the Bible, which constitute about one tenth of the entire text, are beautiful and powerful when read aloud. How this is achieved is discussed in chapter 5, *Upholding the Standard: A New Look at Ancient Poetry.*

Other important issues are covered in chapter 6, *Taking On Sensitive Issues: Careful Consideration of Cultural Concerns*, where a discussion of how the use of nonexclusive language in the *CEV* maintains the Bible's intention of reaching out to all people. Chapter 7, *Helping the Reader: What Besides the Text Makes a Bible Easy To Read and Enjoy?* shows how some additional features which are included in most print editions of the Bible in the *Contemporary English Version* work to aid reader understanding and appreciation of the Bible's message.

Chapter 8, *Conclusion: A New Approach to Bible Translation*, while reiterating many key points made in previous chapters, gives additional attention to the care the translators gave to making sure that the *CEV* is a translation that is a pleasure to read aloud and a joy to hear.

Throughout this book comparisons are made between the ways the *Contemporary English Version* translates specific passages and the way they are handled in more traditional translations. The traditional translations appear in the left hand column(s) and the *Contemporary English Version* in the right hand column (usually marked B or C).

Also included in this book are three appendices. *Appendix A* offers a description of the translation process used in creating the *CEV* and brief biographical information on key personnel. *Appendix B* provides a sampling of texts in the *Contemporary English Version* so that readers can experience for themselves the beauty and clarity of this new translation. *Appendix C* is the official mission statement of the American Bible Society. It provides the context in which all of its translation work is undertaken.

CONTENTS

1
INTRODUCTION:
A TRANSLATION IN THE SPIRIT OF THE
KING JAMES VERSION

Translation it is that opens the window, to let in the light; that breaks the shell, that we may eat the kernel; that puts aside the curtain, that we may look into the most holy place; that removes the cover of the well, that we may come by the water.

"The Translators to the Reader,"
King James Version, 1611

The Significance of the King James Version

It is widely agreed that the most important document in the history of the English language is the *King James Version (KJV)* of the Bible. It would be impossible to measure its spiritual impact on the English speaking world. Historically, many Bible translators have attempted, in some measure, to *retain the form* and much of the familiar language of the *King James Version*. But the translators of the *Contemporary English Version (CEV)* of the Bible have diligently sought to *capture the spirit* of the *King James Version* by following certain principles set forth by its translators in the document "The Translators to the Reader."[1]

The following discussion will show how the translators of the *Contemporary English Version* have attempted to do for the English-speaking world of 1995 what the translators of the *KJV* attempted almost four hundred years ago. In both cases the earnest desire of the translators was to provide God's holy word in the language that people used as they went about their everyday business and conversed among themselves. Both groups of translators knew that the message of the Scriptures was important and worthy of communicating clearly. Later chapters will provide examples and show exactly how the *CEV* translators faced the many challenges of making the ancient Hebrew, Aramaic, and Greek texts understandable to people who read, speak, and hear English today.

---

[1]"The Translators to the Reader was included as a preface in the earliest editions of the *King James Version* Bible. It clearly states the principles followed by the translators commissioned by King James. Over the course of time most publishers of KJV Bibles have chosen not to print this essay. However, it is worthy of examination, and copies are available upon request from the American Bible Society.

"This is the word of God, which we translate."

Accuracy, beauty, clarity, and dignity — all of these can and must be achieved in the translation of the Bible. After all, as the translators of the *King James Version* stated, "This is the word of God, which we translate."

In contemporary American English, the words "inspire" and "inspiration" are often used in the common or everyday sense of something that arouses feelings or emotions. For example, consider the title of one newspaper article: "The Inspiration of Alley Spring." And a frequently used expression in reference to a powerful movie or a significant literary work is, "It's inspiring!" Because the powerful imagery of the Greek word meaning "God-breathed" is not what most people think of when they hear the word "inspired," the translators of the *CEV* preferred to express the meaning of 2 Timothy 3.16 in a way that could be easily understood by readers unfamiliar with traditional biblical language. Where traditional translations say "All Scripture is inspired by God," the *CEV* says directly and clearly, "Everything in the Scriptures is God's Word."

Since this *is* the word of God, the *CEV* translators always took their work seriously. Even so, they have been open to suggestions for improvement. In this regard, the *CEV* remains a "fluid" text, just as the *KJV* has been over the centuries. Making improvements in the text of a translation should not imply that it has been "erroneous." Rather it shows that the translators were aware that as people read the text they felt that certain passages did not communicate the meaning of the Greek or Hebrew clearly enough. As the translators then wrestled to resolve this challenge, they appreciated even more fully the fact that when endeavoring to prepare a faithful translation, the options for expressing a thought or concept are virtually unlimited.

As a matter of fact, there were at least two separate printings of the 1611 *KJV*. Since these differ from one another in so many minute details, it is difficult to determine which was the original. Numerous changes were introduced into later editions of the *KJV*. Most of these were of minor importance, but they were, nevertheless, changes. The phrase "Thou art Christ" (Matthew 16.16) became "Thou art the Christ" (1762), the form that appears in most modern printings of the *KJV*. Similarly, "there is no man good, but one" (Mark 10.18) changed to "there is none good but one" (1638). These are just two examples.

Improvements have been made in the *CEV* as well. An interesting one is found in Galatians 2.9, where the first edition had "these men are supposed to be the *pillars* of the church," which was based on the assumption that the architectural imagery of the Greek text should be maintained. However, "pillar" sounds too much like "pillow." And so when the complete Bible was published, the text was altered to read "these men are supposed to be the backbone of the church." This shift to an anatomical analogy seems to carry more impact for the intended audience of the translation, and there is less opportunity for misunderstanding on the part of the hearer. (For more on how the *CEV* translators give special attention to how words will be heard when read aloud, see chapter 8, p. 72 ff.)

Another interesting change involved the Greek word that appears as "manger" (Luke 2.7,12,16) in most English translations. It was translated "feedbox" in the first edition of the *CEV* New Testament, because (a) "manger" is a technical agricultural term that is not part of the everyday vocabulary of non-rural people; (b) there are too many different definitions for the English word "manger"; (c) "manger" is difficult to "sound out" by an inexperienced reader; and (d) for those who are familiar with the term, it tends to create in the reader's mind a somewhat idyllic "manger scene" that is quite contradictory to the real world into which our Lord was born. However, some users of the *CEV* were opposed to "feedbox." "After all," they argued, "who could sing 'Away in a *Feedbox*'?" Finally, the dilemma was resolved by using "bed of hay" in place of "manger."

As the *KJV* translators observed, the proper translation of a Hebrew or Greek word depends on the context in which the word is used, and so it should not always be translated by the same English word: "Another thing we think good to admonish thee of, gentle reader, that we have not tied ourselves to an uniformity of phrasing or to an identity of words .... For is the kingdom of God become words or syllables? Why should we be in bondage to them, if we may be free? use one precisely when we may use another no less fit as commodiously?" Translating the Word of God in a contemporary style and format can never be a mechanical process of word for word substitution; it requires creative skills and artistry, an understanding and appreciation of current language usage, and absolute dedication to the task of communicating the meaning of the text as clearly as possible.

"We desire that the Scripture . . . may be understood."

That the Scripture may be understood by everyone was a primary goal of the translators of the *King James Version*. And they raised the question, "What can be more [effective toward this goal] than to deliver God's book unto God's people in a tongue which they understand?" Martin Luther also did his German translation of the Bible for the common people, establishing the following guidelines:

> We do not have to inquire of the literal Latin, how we are to speak German . . . . Rather we must inquire about this of the mother in the home, the children on the street, the common man in the marketplace. *We must be guided by their language, the way they speak, and do our translating accordingly.*

Martin Luther draws upon traditional renderings of Matthew 12.34 to demonstrate how common words, if used with uncommon meanings or in uncommon constructions, become obstructions to understanding:

> . . . they will lay [the text] before me literally and translate thus: "Out of the abundance of the heart the mouth speaks." Tell me, is that speaking German? What German could understand something like that? What is "the abundance of the heart"? No German can say that . . .

The same judgment could be made concerning the modern English versions that have "For the mouth speaks what the heart is full of" or "For out of the overflow of the heart the mouth speaks." The individual words themselves are simple enough. The problem is that no one whose first language is English would ever talk that way. In the *CEV* the verse is rendered: "Your words show what is in your heart."

The *CEV* translators knew well the basic translation principle that translators need to *listen* to what they are saying and to realize the possible implications, even of simple words, if placed in unusual order, as in the following where the *CEV* is in the **B** column:

A	**B**
Psalm 45.16	
You will have sons to replace your fathers	Your sons and your grandsons will also be kings
Psalm 68.23	
Then you can stick your *feet* in their blood, and your *dogs* can lick their share.	Then we could stomp on their blood, and our dogs could chew on their bones.
Psalm 78.34	
Anytime he killed them, they would look to him for help; they would come back to God and follow him.	After he killed some of them, the others turned to him with all their hearts.

4

When a modern reader lacks specific knowledge about some aspect of an ancient biblical culture, a literal translation of an idiom can have an undesired comic effect, as in Psalm 40.6:

> But *you have made a hole in my ear*
> to show that my body and life are yours.

Piercing a slave's ear lobe to indicate ownership is a difficult concept to manage effectively in a poetic passage. And this is especially true today, where the practice of voluntary, cosmetic ear piercing for both men and women is common. So in this case the *CEV* substituted the meaning of the act for its form:

> But you made me willing
> to listen and obey.

In order to attain the goals of clarity, beauty, and dignity, the translators of the *CEV* carefully studied every word, phrase, clause, and paragraph of the original. Then, with equal care, they struggled to discover the best way to translate the text, so that it would be suitable both for *private* and *public* reading, and for *memorizing*. The result they have aimed for is an English text that is enjoyable and easily understood by the majority of English speakers, whatever their religious or educational background.

In the *CEV*, economy of words and naturalness of word order combine with clear, direct sentences of comfortable length to facilitate memorization of biblical passages, as in following verses from Proverbs. At the same time, this pattern satisfies the needs for reading aloud to a congregation:

> When someone winks
> or grins behind your back,
>   trouble is on the way. (16.30)

> Controlling your temper
> is better than being a hero
>   who captures a city. (16.32)

> A good reputation and respect
> are worth much more
>   than silver and gold. (22.1)

In poetry, the *appearance of the text on the page* is important, since in oral reading there is a tendency to stress the last word on a line and to pause momentarily before going to the next line, especially when the second line is indented. Compare the three following examples, where the lines of the same text have been broken differently. On the left, the lines have been broken arbitrarily in order to fit as many words as possible on the first line; on the right, lines have been broken carefully in order to preserve the sense units.

Lines Broken Arbitrarily	**Lines Carefully Broken**

(a) He brought me out into a broad
    place.
	(a) He brought me out
	    into a broad place.

b) With the loyal you show yourself
    loyal.
	(b) To the loyal
	    you show yourself loyal.

(c) The LORD, my God, lights up
    my darkness.
	(c) The LORD my God
	    lights up my darkness.

No fault is to be found with the translation itself. Yet there is a significant difference in the *appearance* of the text on the page, because the lines on the right have been *measured*, in order to prevent awkward runovers. In this form, the text not only looks better on the page, but it is easier to read and memorize. And notice how both formats require exactly the same number of lines.

The first translation in the history of the English Bible to develop a text with measured poetry lines is the *CEV*, in which the translators have consciously created a text that will not suffer from awkward line breaks when published in the double-column format most commonly used for Bibles. *Accuracy* is the main concern of translators, but in the translation of biblical poetry, what the reader sees is often what will be *said*, and what others will *hear*. This means that lines improperly broken can easily lead to a misunderstanding of the text, especially for those who must depend upon *hearing* the Scriptures read aloud.

Ancient Hebrew poetry had its own systems of sound, rhyme, and rhythm, as well as a *form* that involves much repetition. It is absolutely impossible in English to retain the sounds, rhymes, and rhythms of the Hebrew text, but traditional translations have attempted to reproduce the frequent repetition, known as parallelism, in which a second line will repeat or expand, either negatively or positively, the thoughts of the previous line. However, this kind of repetition is often ineffective for English speakers unaccustomed to the poetic style of the biblical authors. The use of appositional phrases will confuse English readers rather than bring clarity to the text. Simply put, it masks a Hebrew style in English words. And so, the translators of the *CEV* have followed the guidelines of Martin Luther in the translation of poetry:

Whoever would speak German *must not use Hebrew style.* Rather he must see to it — once he understands the Hebrew author — that he concentrates on the *sense* of the text, asking himself, "Pray tell, what do the Germans say in such a situation?" Once he has the German words to serve his purpose, let him drop the Hebrew words and *express the meaning freely* in the best German he knows.

Among the qualities that critics greatly value in modern English poetry are effortless *economy* and *exactness* of language. It is hoped that readers will discover similar features in the poetry of the *CEV*, which strives for beauty and dignity, without sacrificing accuracy and clarity. In this translation, the poetry often requires fewer lines than is the case in traditional translations, but the *integrity, intent,* and *impact* of the original are consistently maintained. Note, for example, the rendering of Job 38.12-15:

> Did you ever tell the sun to rise?
>   And did it obey?
> Did it take hold of the earth
> and shake out the wicked
>   like dust from a rug?
> <u>Early dawn outlines the hills</u>
> <u>like stitches on clothing</u>
>   <u>or sketches on clay.</u>
> But its light is too much
> for those who are evil,
>   and their power is broken.

The overall intent of the passage is obvious, but of special significance for this discussion is the marked verse: "Early dawn outlines the hills like stitches on clothing or sketches on clay." A more literal rendering would be "The earth takes shape like clay under a seal; its features stand out like those of a garment." In the *CEV* "early dawn" is introduced on the basis of the opening verse that alludes to the dawning of day, while "hills" represents the forms that take shape as the sun rises in the east. A basic problem in the literal rendering is one of word choice, since for most English speakers the first meaning of "seal" is an animal.

The *CEV* has both reversed the order of the imagery of a seal on clay and of the folds on a garment and slightly modified them in order to gain the desired effect. In place of the "imprint of a seal on clay" (as in one modern traditional translation) "sketches on clay" is used; in place of "folds of a garment" the imagery of sewing is substituted: "stitches on clothing." The reason the two items are reversed in the CEV is because it was felt that "sewing" was easier to comprehend than "sketching"; moreover, the poetic effect of this order seems more powerful: "stitches on clothing or sketches on clay." For a more detailed description of poetry in the *CEV*, see chapter 5, p. 47 ff., "Upholding the Standard: A New Look at Ancient Poetry."

In everyday speech, "gender generic" or "inclusive" language is used, because it sounds most natural to people today. This means that where the biblical languages require masculine nouns or pronouns when *both* men and women are intended, this intention must be reflected in translation, though the English *form* may be very different from that of the original. The Greek text of Matthew 16.24 is literally, "If anyone wants to follow me, *he* must deny *himself* and take up *his* cross and follow me." The *CEV* shifts to a form which is still accurate, and at the same time more effective in English: "If any of *you* want to be my followers, *you* must forget about *yourself. You* must take up *your* cross and follow me."

For a more detailed discussion of gender generic language in the *CEV*, see chapter 6, p. 56 ff., "Taking on Sensitive Issues: Careful Consideration of Cultural Concerns."

"Variety of translations is profitable . . ."

The translators of the *King James Version* said, ". . . variety of translations is profitable for the finding out of the sense of the Scriptures." They also stated, "No cause therefore why the Word translated should be denied to be the word, or forbidden to be current, notwithstanding that some imperfections and blemishes may be noted in the setting forth of it."

They went on to make this interesting observation:

> Of one and the same book of Aristotle's *Ethics*, there are extant, not so few as six or seven several translations. Now, if this cost be bestowed upon the gourd, which affords us a little shade, and which today flourishes but tomorrow is cut down, what may we bestow, nay, what ought we not to bestow, on the vine, the fruit whereof makes glad the conscience of man, and the stem thereof abides forever? And this is the Word of God, which we translate.

Each English translation is, in its own right, the Word of God, yet each translation serves to meet the needs of a different audience. In this regard, though it is effective and powerful when read on its own, the *Contemporary English Version* may also be considered a *companion* of traditional translations.

"Of such things that the Spirit of God has left questionable . . ."

Translating the Bible may be compared to living the life of faith. God has not given us all the answers for our pilgrim journey, but we can trust God to guide us along the way. As the translators of the *King James Version* observed:

> . . . it has pleased God in his divine providence here and there to scatter those words and sentences of that difficulty and doubtfulness, not in doctrinal points that concern salvation (for in such it has been vouched that the Scriptures are plain), but in matters of less moment, that fearfulness would better beseem us than confidence . . .

> For as it is a fault of incredulity, to doubt of those things that are evident; so to determine of such things that the Spirit of God has left (even in the mind of the judicious) questionable, can be no less than presumption.

Bible translators do not have the privilege and luxury of working from the original manuscripts of either the Old or New Testament. Indeed, there are numerous difficult passages where decisions must be made concerning what word or words actually belong in the text, and what these words may, in fact, mean. At such places, the translators must choose what seems to be one possible meaning for the difficult text and to indicate this by a note. In fact, this is exactly what the *KJV* translators did: ". . . so diversity of signification and sense [placed] in the margin, where the text is not clear, must needs be good; yea, is necessary." Fortunately, these "words and sentences of that difficulty and doubtfulness" do not in any way leave unclear the central message of the Bible or any of its major doctrines.

Research has shown that the marginal notes in the 1611 edition of the *KJV* numbered 6637 in the Old Testament, of which at least 2156 provided alternative renderings. In the New Testament there were 767 marginal notes, with 582 of them representing alternative renderings. This means that in the two Testaments the translators found the text either "difficult" or "doubtful" in at least 2,738 places!

More recently, the Translations Subcommittee of the United Bible Societies has sponsored projects in which some five thousand textual variants in the ancient manuscripts were analyzed and discussed for the Old Testament, and some two thousand for the New Testament. The translators of the *CEV* benefited enormously from these studies done by specialists in their respective fields. The judgment of the *KJV* translators is still valid: *None* of these passages involve "doctrinal points that concern salvation." However, decisions must be made in each difficult place, even if it involves merely the choice between "<u>R</u>odanim" (רדנים) and "<u>D</u>odanim" (דדנים) in the spelling of a man's name at Genesis 10.4, which has resulted because in Hebrew the letters "R" (r) and "D" (d) look practically alike.

In difficult passages, the *CEV* translators worked on the assumption that originally the text must have made sense and that it was their responsibility to utilize the results of scholarly opinion to produce a text that also makes sense. For example, Psalm 110.3b is acknowledged by Old Testament scholars to be a difficult Hebrew text, but one which had some meaning within the context of the Psalm itself, and that is what the *CEV* translators attempted to accomplish. Compare the two translations of this verse provided below. The one on the left (**A**) makes no connection whatsoever between the two halves of the verse. And the "difficult" second half (marked "b") of the verse neither satisfies the context nor makes any sense on its own. The *CEV* (column **B**) assumes that the two parts of the verse make sense, and it followed scholarly opinion in its restructuring of the total verse:

A	**B**
(a) Your troops will be willing on your day of battle.	(a) Your glorious power will be seen on the day you begin to rule.
(b) Arrayed in holy majesty, from the womb of the dawn you will receive the dew of your youth.	(b) You will wear the sacred robes and shine like the morning sun in all of your strength.

"Having and using as great helps as were needful . . ."

The translators of the *Contemporary English Version* did not attempt to create new or novel understandings of the text. Rather, it was their goal to express accepted understandings of the text in current, everyday English. To do so required *listening* carefully to each word of the biblical text, to the way in which English is spoken today, to the remarks of their reviewers, and especially to the Spirit of God. Once again the comments of the translators of the *King James Version* are appropriate:

Neither did we think much to consult the translators or commentators . . . but neither did we disdain to revise that which we had done, and to bring to the anvil that which we had hammered; but having and using as [many] helps as were needful, and fearing no reproach for slowness, nor coveting praise for expedition, we have at the length, through the good hand of the Lord upon us, brought forth the work to that pass that you see.

Genesis 1.1, 2 will serve to demonstrate how the *CEV* (**B**) is concerned with representing traditional understanding in a creative style and format:

A	B

In the beginning God created the heavens and the earth. Now the earth was formless and empty, darkness was over the surface of the deep, and the Spirit of God was hovering over the waters.	In the beginning God
	created the heavens
	  and the earth.
	The earth was barren
	  with no form of life;
	it was under a roaring ocean
	  covered with darkness.
	But the Spirit of God
	  was moving over the water.

Several important points can be made about the way the translators chose to render these verses. First, the initial sentence ("In the beginning God created the heavens and the earth") represents a traditional, word for word, rendering of the Hebrew text. Such literal renderings are a rare occurrence in the *CEV*. However, in this particular instance, after a number of options were considered, the translators concluded that this was the most poetic and effective of them all. One translation has "the universe" in place of the more descriptive phrase "the heavens and the earth." The *CEV*, on the other hand, retained the figurative expression and supplemented it with a note: "'The heavens and the earth' stood for the universe."

Second, in keeping with contemporary biblical scholarship, the *CEV* provides a note indicating an alternative rendering of the opening words: "Or 'When God began to create the heavens and the earth, the earth was barren with no form of life.'"

Third, the Hebrew phrase translated "Spirit of God" may also mean "a mighty wind," which is indicated by a note as well.

Fourth, the Hebrew conjunction traditionally rendered "And" ("*And* the Spirit . . . ") is legitimately translated "*But*," which more effectively draws the reader's attention to the events to follow.

Fifth, the parallel phrases traditionally rendered "the surface of the deep" and "the waters" are confusing to many people — so confusing, in fact, that at a translation seminar in Thailand a prospective translator said, "Draw me a picture, and I can translate this passage." In the *CEV* the picture is drawn by "telescoping" the two phrases into one: "over the water," which clearly refers back to "ocean."

Finally, but of major importance, is the poetic format that allows the text to make an opening statement of supreme significance:

> In the beginning *God*
> *created* the heavens
> and the earth.

This poetic format consumes more lines than would a prose layout, but it was felt that for the opening verses of the Bible the few extra lines were a worthy investment. (For more about poetry in the *CEV* see chapter 5, p. 47ff., "Upholding the Standard: A New Look at Ancient Poetry.")

"Translation ... opens the window, to let in the light ..."

Because the *CEV* is a careful translation made directly from the ancient language texts and not a paraphrase or modernization of any existing traditional translation, it makes a perfect study companion to any other Bible.

Study Bibles are of many sorts, but a major function in some of them is that of explaining *misleading* or awkward translations, such as "let's attack him with our tongues" (Jeremiah 18.18) or "Can consecrated meat avert [your punishment]?" (Jeremiah 11.15).

Consider the brief statement "in him was life" (John 1.4). First of all, this is *not* a natural English sentence. If it were, other nouns could be substituted for "life," but they cannot without making the statement unintelligible. No matter how long a native speaker of English struggles to understand this rendering of the Greek text into English, the phrase will remain obscure, because its structure does not conform to normal English grammar. New Testament scholars agree that this text means "he is the source of all life," which becomes immediately clear in the *CEV*. The question translators must repeatedly answer is: which is more important — replicating the word order of the Greek text, or providing a word order which is not used in the Greek but which helps the reader grapple with the meaning of the text?

Consider also this line from Hosea 13.14: "Compassion is hidden from my eyes." The LORD is the speaker, and the text means, "I will no longer show compassion" (though it could wrongly be taken to mean "I no longer see anyone showing compassion"). How are readers better assisted — by providing them with imagery so vague that it can be understood in more than one way, or by helping them grapple with the truth conveyed by the imagery?

Ronald Knox, an eloquent Bible translator, states the issue accurately:

> . . . We are sensible of [many] Hebraisms, and most of us would like to see the last of them. But there are hundreds and hundreds of other Hebraisms which we do not notice, because we have allowed ourselves to become accustomed to them. We should have thought it odd if we read in *The Times* . . . "Mr. Churchill then opened his mouth and spoke" – is that English? No, it is a Hebrew idiom clothed in English words.

It is the firm conviction of the *CEV* translators that a Study Bible should not spend major portions of its pages explaining Hebrew idioms that have been expressed in unnatural English phrases. If a so-called "literal" rendering is valuable in the understanding of a particular passage, that information can always be provided in a note. The less space Study Bible editors need to devote to explaining the translation, the more room they will have to explain the historical, cultural, and religious customs that readers need to fully appreciate the Bible's message.

Further observations could be made, but these examples should be sufficient to demonstrate that the *CEV* can serve as an enlightening and insightful companion to other translations, including the time-honored *King James Version* of the Bible. There will certainly always be a place for highly literal translations, especially among scholars learning the ancient languages. But for most English-speaking persons who yearn to understand the meaning of the biblical texts, the *CEV* provides clarity and comprehension. This clears the road for a greater appreciation of the contemporary *relevance* of the text. As the translators of the *KJV* were quick to remind us, it is a good translation "that breaks the shell, that we may eat the kernel." (For more detail on how specific features of the *CEV* aid reader understanding, see chapter 7, p.65 ff., "Helping the Reader: What Besides the Text Makes a Bible Easy To Read and Enjoy?")

This chapter has introduced some of the important features of the *Contemporary English Version*, many of which will be elaborated more fully in the chapters to follow. It is fitting that this chapter concludes with one final quotation from the translators of the *King James Version*:

> It remaineth, that we commend thee to God . . . He removeth the scales from our eyes, the veil from our hearts, opening our wits that we may understand his word, enlarging our hearts, yea correcting our affections, that we may love it above gold and silver, yea that we may love it to the end.

2

FACING THE PROBLEM: MILLIONS OF PEOPLE CAN BARELY READ OR WRITE

More People with Fewer Reading Skills

Almost half of U.S. adults have limited reading and writing skills, according to a study released by the National Center of Education Statistics in 1993. About one-fourth of these ninety million adults with low literacy levels are immigrants who are learning English as a second language. Surprisingly, though, many native speakers of English proved to have some degree of difficulty with reading and writing their own language.

The *Contemporary English Version* is a translation designed with a mission: to be *understood* by people with limited reading skills and *appreciated* by those with advanced literary skills. The head of the department of pediatric neurology in a highly respected medical school of the Northeast says she enjoys the *CEV* "because it is like reading the *New York Times*." A lawyer, who is president of the board of education in a midwestern city, chooses the *CEV* for evening devotions because he doesn't want the hassle of deciphering archaic language in order to understand the meaning of a Scripture passage. And a professor of biblical studies in a southwestern seminary believes this translation will address the minimally educated in a style that will also hold the interest of the most erudite. One reviewer, who did not prefer the *CEV* for his own use because it did not have traditional theological vocabulary, had the following to say:

> It is written for a low reading level and uses simple vocabulary and easily understood sentence structure. Yet, it is not at such a low level that it is jerky and juvenile, like a first grade primer . . . . The narrative sections read like a novel. It is not intimidating, and it has a warm, friendly tone.

The *CEV* began as a project for children and was originally called *Translation for Early Youth*. A basic principle in writing for children is "Do not talk down!" As E.B. White, author of Charlotte's Web, has cautioned: "Anyone who writes down to children is simply wasting his time." So for the first two years of the project careful checking was done with children in grades one through three — and with teachers and parents of children in this age group — to assure that the goals of the translation were being achieved. A detailed analysis was made of the vocabulary, syntax, style, phrase structure, and sentence patterns found in samples of seven different types of books widely used by third graders. Children's reading specialists were recruited to evaluate the style and readability of early drafts of the translation. Finally, for a period of more than two years, the translated texts were tested among adults who possessed limited reading skills and no formal biblical training. As the project progressed, an acclaimed prize-winning poet was retained to review and comment on the text.

This thorough research turned up a number of interesting facts about the way the English language is currently spoken and understood. The following examples will show how the *CEV*, in its effort to speak the language people use in their daily lives, is unique among translations of the Bible.

A Question of "Whom"

In the fourteen hundred pages of children's literature examined, *whom* appeared only once, and the *Oxford English Dictionary* says that this pretentious pronoun is "no longer current in unstudied colloquial speech." A letter from an Australian reviewer was the first to call this fact to the attention of the translators, when he noted that "whom" was hardly ever used in his country.

Another letter, this time from a professor in a university on the west coast, offered further encouragement to ban this pronoun from the *CEV*:

> When I told my introductory journalism class ... that perhaps "whom" was outdated, they let out a cheer. It seems learning the "who" versus "whom" distinction still eludes many students.

In both spoken and *written* English *who* is properly used in constructions such as this headline from a North Carolina newspaper: "*Who* Do You Really Trust?" And it would be the height of the ridiculous to come up behind someone and shout, "Guess *whom!*" Consequently, "whom" is absent from the *CEV*, and so Jesus asks the mob sent to arrest him, "*Who* are you looking for?" (John 18.5).

The Use of "The"

For the most part, modern translations of the Bible no longer use the ancient pronoun forms *thee* or *thou* or *thy*, though many continue to use the definite article *the* in places quite unnatural for everyday spoken English.

The *Contemporary English Version*, which is concerned equally with accuracy and aesthetics, has given close attention to such matters, as in Job 39.5, 6 (*CEV* is in column **B**):

A	**B**
Who let *the* wild donkey go free?	Who set wild donkeys free?
Who untied *his* ropes?	I alone help them survive
I gave *him* the wasteland as *his* home,	in salty desert sand.
the salt flats as *his* habitat.	

It is true that American English may use "*the* wild donkey" as a classification for wild donkeys in general, which is precisely what the Hebrew form means. However, when this expression is immediately followed by the pronouns *his* and *him*, the reader's first inclination is to think of *one specific donkey* that someone let free, whether accidentally or intentionally. This is not confusing in the *CEV*, because the plural form "wild donkeys" is used.

Many other examples are possible, such as "though *the* fig tree does not bud" (Habakkuk 3.17) and "Wherever there is a dead body, *the* vultures will gather" (Matthew 24.28). Perhaps the most interesting occurrence of this use of *the* appears in Matthew 26.34 (Mark 14.30; Luke 22.34; John 13.38), which has traditionally been translated: "before *the* rooster crows." The problem is that in English usage "*the* rooster" implies either (a) a previously mentioned rooster, or (b) the only available rooster, or (c) a designated rooster, when in actual fact the meaning is either "before roosters start crowing" or "before *a* rooster crows," as in the *CEV*.

"Through" It All

The use of *through* with persons or abstract nouns has been rejected by the *CEV* translators because doing something "*through* someone" is an extremely difficult linguistic concept for many people to process. This is why the *CEV* does not render the opening verses of Hebrews in the manner of one modern translation which says "through the prophets ... through his Son ... through whom." Instead, this passage is rendered as follows:

> Long ago in many ways and at many times God's prophets spoke his message to our ancestors. But now at last God sent his Son to bring his message to us. God created the universe by his Son, and everything will someday belong to the Son.

The only exception to this rule is found in Genesis 42.23: "They did not know that Joseph could understand them, since he was speaking *through* an interpreter." But it was felt that the complete phrase "through an inter-preter" would be easily grasped, especially by persons who are learning English as a second language.

Brothers, Sisters, and Friends

Brothers, when referring collectively to a group consisting of both men and women, was felt to be inappropriate for use in the *CEV*. In fact, this word does not appear except when the context makes it clear that a familial relationship is intended. For a more detailed discussion of gender generic language, see chapter 6, p. 56 ff., "Taking on Sensitive Issues: Careful Consideration of Cultural Concerns."

"Awesome" and "Totally"

Though once a powerful adjective used to describe the respect felt for God, the word "awesome" has no place in the *CEV*. In contemporary society the term is used of so many trivial things, including pizzas and soft drinks, that it has lost its impact.

Similarly, "totally" has lost much of its original power and is now used, especially by young people, to modify almost anything: "totally radical" or "totally cool" or "totally different." Neither "totally" nor "awesome" will be found in the *CEV*.

The Use of "None" as a Plural Form

Perhaps of lesser consequence are the occasional questions raised regarding *none* as a plural form in the *CEV*. However, it does deserve a brief explanation. The *American Heritage Dictionary* points out: "It should be noted that *none* has for centuries been used by the best writers as if it were a plural form, taking both plural verbs and plural pronouns . . . ." Accordingly, the *CEV* uses either singular or plural forms, but *none* is never used as both plural and singular within the same passage. There is also the matter of *style* in making the choice between a singular and plural form, as in Isaiah 40.26, where the *CEV* opted for the plural form, simply because "*none* of the stars *are*" sounds better than "*none* of the stars *is*":

> The LORD is so powerful
> that none of the stars
> are ever missing

The Absence of "Woe"

Early into this project a reviewer criticized the *CEV* because of its handling of the Hebrew word often rendered *woe* in English translations. However, "woe" is merely an attempt to imitate the *sound* of the Hebrew word, rather than to communicate its *meaning*. For English speakers, the *sound* of the word is problematic because of the word "Whoa" which is pronounced identically. This will cause confusion for those who must depend upon hearing the Scriptures read: "Woe! Woe, O great city" (Revelation 18.10,15,19) will inevitably sound like "Whoa! Whoa, O great city" to the person uninitiated into the mysterious world of biblical language.

The Hebrew (and Greek) word can be an expression of pain, anger, horror, pity, disaster, or calamity, and the *CEV* attempts to represent these meanings properly as the different contexts dictate. Needless to say, a variety of terms and phrases are used, among them: "You are in for trouble" or "You are doomed."

Southern Desert and Northern Syria

In place of merely "sounding out" the technical Hebrew term *Negeb* ("dry southern region"), the *CEV* uses "Southern Desert," as in "Abram started out toward the Southern Desert" (Genesis 12.9) and "... the Amalakites live in the Southern Desert" (Numbers 13.29).

For *Aram-Naharaim*, the *CEV* translates "northern Syria," with a major note at Genesis 24.10:

> **northern Syria**: *The Hebrew text has "Aram-Naharaim," probably referring to the land around the city of Haran (see also "Paddan-Aram" in 25.20; 28.2,6; 31.18,20; 33.18; 35.23-26; 46.8-15; and "Paddan" in 48.7).*

In Hosea 12.12 "Jacob escaped to Syria" is followed by a note:

> **Syria**: *The Hebrew text has "Aram," probably referring to northern Syria in the region of Haran.*

Footnotes and a Mini Dictionary for the Bible that appear in most editions of the *CEV* Bible will help readers who may be familiar with traditional biblical names to identify these places on maps and in the narratives.

Hebrew Names and Family Ancestry

There are a number of places where the Hebrew text will use the formula *son of ... son of ... son of* when making a list of a person's ancestors. This can be distracting or tiresome for modern English speakers. Providing a list of a person's male ancestors may have been important information to the writer and to the original readers, but often this is not of much immediate value to the contemporary user of the text.

The *CEV* attempts to minimize the difficulty, while remaining faithful to the intent of a passage. For instance, in Zephaniah 1.1 the Hebrew text has "Zephaniah son of Cushi son of Gedaliah son of Amariah son of Hezekiah," which *CEV* represents as "Zephaniah, the son of Cushi, the grandson of Gedaliah, the great-grandson of Amariah, and the great-great-grandson of Hezekiah." On occasion, some of these identifiers can be transferred to a note: In Jeremiah 39.14, where the Hebrew text has "Gedaliah son of Ahikam son of Shaphan," the *CEV* renders "Gedaliah son of Ahikam" with a note: "*son of Ahikam*: Hebrew 'son of Ahikam and grandson of Shaphan.'"

In contexts where a lengthy series of ancestral identifiers are found, this technique of placing them in the footnotes is extremely helpful, especially when it is done in combination with other kinds of restructuring, as in **B**. The passage is Numbers 27.1:

A	**B**
Then the daughters of Zelophehad came forward. Zelophehad was the son of Hepher son of Gilead son of Machir son of Manasseh son of Joseph, a member of the Manassite clans. The names of his daughters were: Mahlah, Noah, Hoglah, Milcah, and Tirzah.	Zelophehad was from the Manasseh tribe, and he had five daughters, whose names were Mahlah, Noah, Hoglah, Milcah, and Tirzah.

In the *CEV* (column **B**), the ancestral names are supplied in a note:

> 27.1 **Zelophehad**: *Hebrew "Zelophehad son of Hepher son of Gilead son of Machir son of Manasseh son of Joseph."*

More than Words

Although individual words are important, the matter of word order and word combinations are in some respects even more important. The meaning of an unknown word can often be understood from the context in which it occurs — if the phrase, clause, and sentence order reflect everyday usage. On the other hand, even an ordinary word can become problematic when used with a specialized meaning. Such a word is the verb "call" in its technical Christian sense. Consequently the word "choose" is often the preferred way of translating this word in the *CEV*: "My friends, you must do all you can to show that God has really *chosen* and selected you." (2 Peter 1.10).

Unnatural word order can function as an effective literary device if skillfully employed. But it is unsettling when the order is merely the result of careless restructuring. The following example from Psalm 105.23 shows how confusion can result when greater care is not taken: "Then Israel entered

Egypt; Jacob lived as an alien in the land of Ham." In the Hebrew text "Israel" and "Jacob" are different ways of referring to the people of Israel, while "Egypt" and "Ham" each refer to the country of Egypt. And for modern readers there is the additional problem of the term "alien," which for most people today signifies a creature from another planet. All of these are common words, but their cumulative effect is to cause confusion for the ordinary reader and hearer.

When translators are crafting a text to be read aloud, sentence order is a more important consideration than sentence length (see the next section). Inverting the natural order of speaker/speech may occasionally enliven the text, if handled with sensitivity. But when this is not skillfully done, the result can be confusing for those who must depend upon hearing the Scriptures, as two consecutive verses from a traditional translation of Matthew 17.25, 26 will demonstrate. When reading this, keep in mind that the *quotation* marks and *commas* are silent:

> "Of course," Peter answered. . . .
> "The foreigners," answered Peter.

The traditional rendering of Acts 15.16-18 in column **A** below is no less frustrating to the reader than to the hearer — all because the text has not been restructured in what would be considered a natural pattern for spoken English. Compare this with the *CEV* in column **B**.

A	B
'After this I will return	"I, the Lord, will return
and rebuild David's fallen tent.	and rebuild
Its ruins I will rebuild,	David's fallen house.
and I will restore it,	I will build it from its ruins
that the remnant of men may seek the	and set it up again.
Lord,	Then other nations
and all the Gentiles who bear my	will turn to me
name,	and be my chosen ones.
says the Lord, who does these things'	I, the Lord, say this.
that have been known for ages.	I promised it long ago."

Sentence Length

Sentence length is not an absolute measure of readability. However, reading specialists agree that a high frequency of long, involved sentences tends to decrease the intelligibility of a text. For example, one translation of 2 Peter 2.4-9 is comprised of one overlong sentence containing five "if" clauses, one parenthetical statement, one statement set off by dashes, two "but" clauses — plus several more clauses introduced by other terms: "when," "then," "who," "and," "while," and "for." The word count totals one hundred fifty-one, and in one setting the sentence occupies twenty-one lines on the page. In the CEV this passage is restructured into three paragraphs and nine sentences. Each sentence flows naturally from the one that precedes it, and readers are never forced to "go back" in order to pick up the strand of an earlier thought.

Slang

The translators of the *CEV* were always careful *not* to incorporate slang or street jargon into the text. Preliminary checking showed that even young people would appreciate language that does not attempt either to "imitate" or "talk down" to them. Slang and street jargon tend to belong to subgroups rather than wide audiences, and it usually becomes dated much more quickly than other terms in general everyday use. Even the word "peace" has taken on too many conflicting connotations, and so the *CEV* uses other ways of expressing a greeting. This is illustrated in the verse describing how Jesus appears to his disciples after being raised from death: "Suddenly, Jesus appeared in the middle of the group. He *greeted* them and showed them his hands and his side." (John 20.19b- 20a).

Audience Sensitivity

Audience sensitivity is of absolute importance in the communication of meaning, and it is the job of the translators to make themselves aware of the special needs of their intended audience. The *CEV* was translated primarily for persons who (a) know a minimum of church language, (b) have limited biblical knowledge and limited reading skills, and (c) whose primary contact with the text may come by hearing it read aloud. Since this audience may be largely *outside* the church, the translators of the *CEV* felt it their mission to be sure that the words and phrasing used in the *CEV* are the ones the majority of the people in the general culture would understand. In this way the *CEV* should successfully meet the need of all English-speaking people, whether they are part of a worshiping community or not.

Research has also shown that there is another kind of illiteracy facing people who want to share God's word with others — biblical illiteracy. Many people are ignorant of simple facts about the Bible, such as the names of the four Gospels or even several of the Apostles. Even within churches the level of knowledge about the Scriptures is shrinking. In trying to help combat this problem, the translators of the *CEV* have worked hard to create a translation that meets people where they are. It does this in a number of ways.

Helping the Reader Understand "Difficult Books"

In research among Bible readers, it was discovered that some books are read much less often than others, because they appear archaic and technical in nature and seem less relevant to modern life. In fact, this excuse for not reading the Bible has been given its own name — the "Leviticus Syndrome." But the translators of the *CEV* were as much concerned about reader appeal in the opening verses of Leviticus as they were in the prologue to the Gospel of John. However, like each book of the Bible, Leviticus posed its own set of problems to the translators.

The *format* of the *CEV* Leviticus is in every respect designed to be "user-friendly," as may be observed by the layout of chapter one:

> [1-3]The LORD spoke to Moses from the sacred tent and gave him instructions for the community of Israel to follow when they offered sacrifices.
>
> ### Sacrifices To Please the LORD
>
> *The LORD said:*
> Sacrifices to please me must be completely burned on the bronze altar.
> Bulls or rams or goats are the animals to be used for these sacrifices. If the animal is a bull, it must not have anything wrong with it. Lead it to the entrance of the sacred tent, and I will let you know if it is acceptable to me.

The opening three verses (1-3) have been combined and restructured to allow for easier readability. The use of descriptive section headings and the italicized phrase "*The LORD said*" make it clear who is speaking and what subjects are being addressed. Not only is the structure of Leviticus difficult in some traditional translations, but the unfamiliar sacrificial terminology can have a discouraging impact upon the average reader. The term "a *burnt* offering" used in traditional translations is quite foreign to modern religious life and worship.

Instead of retaining the technical terms for the different kinds of sacrifices in the Old Testament, the *CEV* has translated the sacrifices according to their *function* rather than their *form*. Footnotes are added to further explain what has been done. For example, following "Sacrifices to please me" is the note:

1.1-3 **Sacrifices to please me:** *These sacrifices have traditionally been called "whole burnt offerings" because the whole animal was burned on the altar. A main purpose of such sacrifices was to please the LORD with the smell of the offering, and so in the CEV they are often called "sacrifices to please the LORD."*

Other sacrifices are dealt with in a similar fashion and are accompanied by notes: "Grain offerings" have become "sacrifices to give thanks to the LORD," while "peace offerings" or "offerings of well-being" are now "sacrifices to ask the LORD's blessing."

In conclusion, it cannot be stated too often that the *Contemporary English Version* is a translation with a clear mission — to reach people with the message of the Scriptures in language that is clear, easy to understand, and natural to the ear. In a time when people are reading less and are relying increasingly on electronic forms of communication, it is essential that any Bible they read or hear read from the pulpit echoes the natural rhythms and vocabulary of everyday speech.

3

FINDING SOLUTIONS:
USING LANGUAGE PEOPLE CAN UNDERSTAND

"The War on Gobbledygook"

A recent article in the financial section of a well-known weekly magazine was titled, "The War on Gobbledygook," and it dealt with the growing need "to translate" the "typically dense" data on stocks and bonds "into simple English." Similar needs have been felt in the fields of law, medicine, and insurance, to mention only a few.

In light of a 1994 poll by the Barna Research Group, "Christian churches are preaching their message in terms that most people don't understand." Their observations were alarming, to say the least. With regard to John 3.16 they noted: "Overall 65 percent of the general population and 50 percent of born-again Christians said they did not know what the term 'John 3.16' meant." Worst of all, those who come to the Scriptures, seeking answers to problems, are sometimes turned off by words and phrases that have no meaning. Many of these terms come from a long religious tradition and are cherished by believers who grew up reading traditional Bible translations. They include heavy theological nouns like *justification, righteousness, redemption, atonement, sanctification, and repentance.* What few people realize is that many of these terms were brought into the English Bible by John Wycliffe (c.1328–1384) from the Latin Bible. Wycliffe was a Latin scholar who knew little Creek.

In addition to these technical terms are phrases that have been called "Biblicisms" because they have no independent meaning apart from their place in traditional Bible translations and prayers, and the hymns that are based on these translations. Biblicisms are especially frustrating to the uninitiated. In fact, even persons who are "familiar" with this mysterious code still cannot always decipher their meaning: "Grace is poured upon your lips" (Psalm 45.2); "You stiff-necked people, with uncircumcised hearts and ears!" (Acts 7.51); "a kind of firstfruits of all he created" (James 1.18); "those who have fallen asleep in him" (1 Thessalonians 4.14). In each of these texts the meaning is impaired rather than clarified by the quaintness of the translations.

No translation can be said to be without *any* traditional theological terminology. This is because translating is never done in a vacuum, and translators must always consider the sensitivities of the Christian communities that will use and distribute the translation. However, if a translation is to be used effectively to communicate God's message to people who have never heard it before, it is important that it be as free of insiders' jargon and technical terminology as possible.

The remainder of this chapter will demonstrate how some traditional theological terms were dealt with in the *CEV* and how certain sensitive issues were faced.

1. The Question of Grace

The English word *grace* comes from the Latin word *gratia*, the translation of the Greek word *charis*. Evidently, the expression "grace of God" did not enter the English language until A.D. 1175, which was more than eleven centuries after the apostle Paul wrote his letters to the Christians at Rome. As the translators of the *King James Version* pointed out, words are *not* "images to be worshiped." And one of the first responsibilities of a Bible translator is to *listen* to the way words are *currently* used by the intended audience.

Even before the publication of the *CEV* New Testament in May, 1991, careful study and observation were applied to the way *grace* has been used in newspapers, magazines, and books, as well as on radio and television. The real questions translators must answer for themselves in order to prepare a text that will not be misunderstood by people today are (a) How is "grace" used in everyday life and (b) how will it be understood by someone unfamiliar with typical church language?

A review of the contexts of *grace* in current usage is revealing. The ballet dancer Beckah Voight is "*grace* in motion" *(News Leader)*. The blues singer Billie Holiday is "a charismatic interpretive artist touched with *grace*" *(Publisher's Weekly)*. The actress Audrey Hepburn was said to be "a spirit of regal *grace*" *(Time)*. Jacqueline Kennedy Onassis "confronts cancer with *grace*" *(People Magazine)*. The tennis player Arthur Ashe "died as he lived, with *grace* and dignity" (Connie Chung, CBS News). Television commercials celebrate the "fluid *grace*" of the Seville Cadillac, and the "beauty, elegance, *grace*" of the Rolex watch. Norman Maclean *(A River Runs Through It)* remarks that "All good things come by *grace*, and *grace* comes by art..."

Every occurrence of *grace* in these examples from current usage has the meaning of "a pleasing quality, attractiveness, seemingly effortless beauty or charm." This is why it is impossible to create an everyday English sentence by using *grace* in the biblical sense of "you are saved by *grace*." This also explains why pastors often feel that *grace* requires an explanation even to Christians. As a matter of fact, one prominent minister stated, "I never use *grace* from the pulpit, without explaining what I mean."

Now, in light of this likely misunderstanding, how will the average reader understand "full of *grace*" (John 1.14), "*grace* for *grace*" (John 1.16), "great *grace* was upon them all" (Acts 4.33), "throne of *grace*" (Hebrews 4.16), "spirit of *grace* (Hebrews 10.29), and "God of all *grace*" (1 Peter 5.10)?

In the Greek-speaking world of the first century A.D., the Greek word *charis*, which traditional translations render as *grace*, could be used in at least three different ways: (a) "seemingly effortless beauty or charm" (as in current English), (b) "an act of showing (undeserved) kindness," and (c) "a response to or the result of an act of kindness." In the New Testament *charis* occurs predominantly in the second sense, with God as the one who shows kindness. The third meaning is also used with some frequency, especially in the sense of "thanks." But the first meaning is found only a few times, for example, Luke 4.22 ("amazed at the gracious words") and Colossians 4.6 ("Let your speech always be gracious").

Finding a suitable way of translating *charis* into contemporary English was a special challenge in the course of crafting the *CEV* New Testament text, one that called for much careful thought and innovative skill. For years theologians have defined the English term *grace* as "God's unmerited favor," which, if properly understood, conveys accurately the most frequent meaning of *charis* in the New Testament. While this is a fairly succinct way of defining *grace*, its suitability in a contemporary English translation of the Bible is limited. First, the word "unmerited" is a rather high level term that is not widely used in everyday speech. Second, "favor" frequently implies something trivial and most often appears in constructions such as, "Will you do me a favor?" Also, in certain contexts "favor" may suggest partiality or favoritism. Third, the translators recognized that specialized meanings are not easily imposed upon words in general use. Fourth, a translation into contemporary English must reflect, rather than dictate, the meanings of words.

With this in mind, observe in the following examples how carefully the *CEV* New Testament text has been crafted in order to communicate precisely the intended meaning of *charis*.

Traditional Translations	Contemporary English Version

Acts 4.33

With great power the apostles continued to testify to the resurrection of the Lord Jesus, and much grace was upon them all.

In a powerful way the apostles told everyone that the Lord Jesus was now alive. God greatly blessed his followers ...

Romans 6.1

What shall we say, then? Shall we go on sinning so that grace may increase?

What should we say? Should we keep on sinning, so that God's wonderful kindness will show up even better?

Galatians 1.15, 16

But when God, who set me apart from birth and called me by his grace, was pleased to reveal his Son in me so that I might preach him among the Gentiles, I did not consult any man ...

But even before I was born, God had chosen me. He was kind and had decided to show me his Son, so that I would announce his message to the Gentiles. I didn't talk this over with anyone.

Hebrews 4.16

Let us then approach the throne of grace with confidence, so that we may receive mercy and find grace to help us in our time of need.

So whenever we are in need, we should come bravely before the throne of our merciful God. There we will be treated with undeserved kindness, and we will find help.

Hebrews 12.15

See to it that no one misses the grace of God and that no bitter root grows up to cause trouble and defile many.

Make sure that no one misses out on God's wonderful kindness. Don't let anyone become bitter and cause trouble for the rest of you.

The *Contemporary English Version*, in the spirit of the *KJV*, does not assume that the English term *grace* adequately expresses the meaning of the Greek term *charis*. In the *King James Version* "favor" was sometimes used (Luke 1.30; 2.52; Acts 2.47; 7.10), as was "thank" or "thanks" (Luke 6.32-34 [three occurrences]; 17.9; 2 Corinthians 2.14). In 1 Corinthians 16.3 the *KJV* translators preferred "liberality," and in 2 Corinthians 8.4 they chose "gift." Significant are the two occurrences of *charis* in 1 Peter 2.19, 20, where the first is translated "thankworthy" ("For this is thankworthy") and the second "acceptable" ("this is acceptable to God"). Romans 3.24-26 will demonstrate how the *CEV* (column **C**) has dealt with the term *grace*, as well as other difficult conceptual terms *(justification, redemption, atonement,* and *righteousness,* and *forbearance,* as well as *through* (of persons and abstract nouns) in a single passage. Two traditional translations (columns **A** and **B**) are included for comparison:

A	B	C
[24](All) are justified freely by his grace through the redemption that came by Christ Jesus. [25]God presented him as a sacrifice of atonement, through faith in his blood. He did this to demonstrate his justice, because in his forbearance he had left the sins committed beforehand unpunished — [26]he did it to demonstrate his justice at the present time, so as to be just and the one who justifies those who have faith in Jesus.	[24]But by the free gift of God's grace all are put right with him through Christ Jesus, who sets them free. [25-26]God offered him, so that by his blood he should become the means by which people's sins are forgiven through their faith in him. God did this in order to demonstrate that he is righteous. In the past he was patient and overlooked people's sins; but in the present time he deals with their sins, in order to demonstrate his righteousness. In this way God shows that he himself is righteous and that he puts right everyone who believes in Jesus.	[24]God treats us much better than we deserve, and because of Christ Jesus, he freely accepts us and sets us free from our sins. [25-26]God sent Christ to be our sacrifice. Christ offered his life's blood, so that by faith in him we could come to God. And God did this to show that in the past he was right to be patient and forgive sinners. This also shows that God is right when he accepts people who have faith in Jesus.

2. Justification and Righteousness

Another difficult word that will not be found in the *CEV* is *justification,* and its related terms *justify* and *righteousness.* Because of the importance of this concept in Jewish and Christian theology, intensive thought and research went into the preparation of the translation. Many scholars see its background in the legal system of New Testament times. At that time a person was considered *justified* when pronounced *not guilty.* However, *justify* and *justification* are not used in this way in American courts of law. When asked what these terms signify in the legal system, an attorney replied, "Exactly what they do in everyday, spoken English; they have no specialized meaning." In most instances the word is used in its usual sense of either making an excuse or giving a rationale for someone's action.

Whether legal terms or not, the apostle Paul uses these to describe something at the very core of the divine-human relationship, and so a search began for a word or phrase that would best convey the essence of this concept. Finally, the notion of "acceptance" was decided upon, because everyone is in basic agreement that when God "justifies" someone, God is accepting that guilty person because of what Jesus has done. The pastor of a large church in the Midwest confirmed this in a sermon: "You are guilty, and God says, 'I *accept* you as though you had never sinned.' That's what we mean by justification."

It is helpful to see how these important terms are dealt with in Romans 3.20-24 of the *CEV*:

> ²⁰God doesn't *accept* people simply because they obey the Law ... ²¹Now we see how God does *make us acceptable* to him. The Law and the Prophets tell how we *become acceptable* . . . . ²²God treats everyone alike. He *accepts* people only because they have faith in Jesus Christ . . . ²⁴ . . . and because of Christ Jesus, he freely *accepts* us and sets us free from our sins.

This notion of "acceptance" is scattered throughout the Old Testament, whether in reference to actions or foods, people or sacrifices, that are either "acceptable" or "unacceptable" to God. This connection to the Old Testament provides the Bible student with an excellent clue for understanding this important idea in Paul's letters.

In addition it should be noted that the same Greek word usually rendered *justification* sometimes appears in traditional translations as *righteousness* (Romans 6.19). Because *righteous* in contemporary English usage is most often taken to mean possessing the innate qualities of *goodness* and *virtue*, it is likewise not used by the *CEV* translators when rendering this Greek term. A good example of how this was dealt with in the *CEV* appears in the discussion of Romans 6.19 in the following section on *Sanctification*.

3. Sanctification

For the most part *sanctify* and *sanctification* have to do with either belonging to God in a unique sense or sharing in the character (specifically the "holiness") of God, both of which are difficult concepts to express. And so where the Greek is literally "Sanctify them in the truth; your word is truth" *CEV* has "Your word is the truth. So let this truth make them completely yours" (John 17.17). Similarly, "for their sakes I sanctify myself, so that they may also be sanctified in truth" in CEV is "I have given myself completely for their sake, so that they may belong completely to the truth" (John 17.19). In 1 Thessalonians 5.23 ("May the God of peace sanctify you entirely") the *CEV* uses the word "holy" to express this concept: "I pray that God, who gives peace, will make you completely holy."

Both *righteousness* (meaning *justification*) and *sanctification* appear in Romans 6.19: "present your members as slaves of righteousness for sanctification". In this passage the *CEV* shifts away from heavy noun constructions which are difficult and abstract in English. Taking *righteousness* as a reference to the *righteous* demands of God, the *CEV* renders this phrase as follows: "But now you must make every part of your body serve God, so that you will belong completely to him." *Sanctification* in this example is captured by the phrase "you will belong completely to him." Even more restructuring is required in 1 Peter 3.15, where the Greek could be literally translated "In your hearts sanctify Christ as Lord." The *CEV* reads "Honor Christ and let him be the Lord of your life."

4. Redemption

In Matthew 20.28 (Mark 10.45) the Greek word rendered *redeem* by many translations is translated *rescue* by the *CEV*: "The Son of Man did not come to be a slave master, but a slave who will give his life to rescue many people." A note accompanies the text:

> **rescue**: *The Greek word often, though not always, means the payment of a price to free a slave or a prisoner.*

The *CEV* also uses "rescue" in several other passages (Galatians 3.13; 1 Timothy 2.6; 2 Peter 2.1; Revelation 14.3,4). Other passages require different phrasing. Galatians 4.5 has "set (us) free (from the Law)", while 2 Peter 2.1 reads "*paid a great price* for them" in place of the more traditional "redeemed them."

5. Atonement

Like the concepts of justification and sanctification, the important concept of *atonement* has deep roots in Jewish religious practice as described in the Old Testament. As with the previous terms discussed, atonement is not readily understood by the average person on the street. *Make an atonement* is equivalent to "offer a sacrifice to take away sins" as in the following *CEV* examples from the Old Testament book most associated with the Jewish sacrificial system, Leviticus:

> "Lay your hand on its head, and I will accept the animal as a sacrifice for taking away your sins" (Leviticus 1.4)

> "By his sacrifice the sin of the whole nation will be forgiven" (Leviticus 4.21)

Similarly, the important Jewish holy day, the Day of Atonement (Yom Kippur, Leviticus 23.27, 28; 25.9) appears as the Great Day of Forgiveness in the *CEV*. A Mini Dictionary for the Bible found in most editions of the *CEV* Bible helps the reader understand this festival day in relation to the more traditional term still used by Jews today.

The sense of sacrifice is equally important in understanding New Testament occurrences of the Greek word traditionally translated *atonement*. The difficult clause "whom God put forward as a sacrifice of atonement by his blood, effective through faith" (Romans 3.25) is translated in the *CEV* as "God sent Christ to be our sacrifice. Christ offered his life's blood, so that by faith in him we could come to God." And in Hebrews 2.17 "make a sacrifice of atonement for the sins of the people" is rendered "sacrifice himself for the forgiveness of our sins." And in 1 John 2.2 "He is the atoning sacrifice for our sins" is rendered "Christ is the sacrifice that takes away our sins." In each case the emphasis is on the fact that Christ gave his life in order to secure God's forgiveness.

6. Repentance

Depending on the context and the persons addressed, *repent (repentance)* is translated in the *CEV* as either "turn back to God" or "turn to God." Repentance for many people today calls to mind images of doomsday prophets. While people today may recognize that a change is being called for, they may see only what one is called to turn from (sin), and not what one is called to turn to (God). In another place the complex construction "baptism of repentance for the forgiveness of your sins" was restructured by making two sentences: "Turn back to God and be baptized! Then your sins will be forgiven" (Mark 1.4).

7. Covenant and Gospel

For the readership of *CEV* it was felt that the more familiar word *agreement* was better suited than the rather sophisticated term *covenant*: "This is my blood, and with it God makes his *agreement* with you" (Matthew 26.28).

The use of "good news" *(CEV)* as a translation of the Greek word for *gospel (euangelion)* goes back at least to Edgar J. Goodspeed's *An American Translation* of 1923. Though not all translators since that time have followed his cue, it is difficult to find a better choice.

8. Kingdom of God (Heaven)

The term *kingdom of God or kingdom of heaven* occurs more than a hundred times in the Greek New Testament, and since the concept is so prevalent in the Old Testament as well, the term was retained for the most part in the *CEV* New Testament. Two examples will suffice: "God's kingdom will soon be here" (Mark 1.15) and "God blesses those people who depend only on him. They belong to the kingdom of heaven" (Matthew 5.3).

There were, however, a few places in the New Testament where it was decided that the text of the *CEV* would be clearer if the Greek phrase were rendered by using familiar English idioms. In Matthew 6.33 "Seek first his kingdom" was rendered "Put God's work first." In Matthew 19.12 "for the sake of the kingdom of heaven" was rendered "in order to serve God better." Only minor restructuring was usually done elsewhere: "The kingdom of God is not food and drink" was rendered "God's kingdom isn't about eating and drinking" (Romans 14.17); "the kingdom of God depends not on talk" became "God's kingdom isn't just a lot of words" (1 Corinthians 4.20); "inherit the kingdom of God," which occurs several times in the New Testament, is usually translated "share in God's kingdom" (1 Corinthians 6.10; 15.50; Galatians 5.21). In Ephesians 5.5, where the Greek might be literally "... has no inheritance in the kingdom of Christ and of God," the *CEV* translates it "... will never be part of the kingdom that belongs to Christ and God."

The Mini Dictionary for the Bible that accompanies some editions of the *CEV* Bible provides a concise but helpful definition for *God's Kingdom*: God's rule over people, both in this life and in the next.

9. Anoint

In ancient Israel, when people were chosen to be either kings or priests or prophets, there was usually a ceremony in which they were "anointed" by having olive oil poured over their head. Since *anoint* is not used with this same specialized sense in modern society, it is usually translated according to its meaning: "He has *chosen* me to tell the good news" (Luke 4.18). Several Old Testament passages where the word occurs are accompanied by a note, giving an explanation of the ceremony, as in Zechariah 4.14:

> **chosen leaders:** *The Hebrew text has "people of oil." In ancient times prophets, priests, and kings had olive oil poured over their heads to show that they had been chosen (see 1 Samuel 10.1; 16.13).*

10. Hosanna

Hosanna (Matthew 21.9,15; Mark 11.9, 10; John 12.13) is technically not a translation but a "sounding out" of a Hebrew word (carried over into Greek), which means something like "please save us." In the *CEV* it is represented by "Hooray" with a note: "This translates a word that can mean 'please save us.' But it is most often used as a shout of praise to God."

11. Synagogue

Synagogue does not appear in the *CEV* — instead, the Greek word is translated "Jewish meeting place" or "Jewish meeting," depending upon the context. Although "synagogue" is a fairly well-known word, it is almost impossible to "sound out" by new readers, which is one of the many groups the translators hope to reach with this easy-to-read translation.

12. Titles for Church Leadership

Since the *CEV* is intended for persons who may have no more than a minimal knowledge of "church language," it was decided to translate *deacon* and *bishop* and *elder (presbyter)* with more general terms. This also resolved the problems resulting from the specific meanings these terms have developed within various denominations. The following samples show how these terms are typically rendered, without suggesting that any one position is either "higher" or "lower" than the others: "deacon" is usually "officer" (Philippians 1.1; 1 Timothy 3.8,10,12,13), though "leader" is also used (Romans 16.1); "bishop" is "official" (Philippians 1.1; 1 Timothy 3.1, 2,4; Titus 1.7); and "elder" is "(church) leader" (1 Timothy 5.17,19; Titus 1.5). In Acts 20.28 the traditional word for "bishop" is translated according to its function: "everyone the Holy Spirit has placed in your care."

13. Parables

Today New Testament scholars frequently use *story* when speaking about the *parables* of Jesus as the following quotation will demonstrate:

> For our purposes, what is of special interest in the parables of Jesus is not only that he told *stories*, but that the *stories* were so human and realistic. To press these images is to pull the *stories* out of shape and to weaken their thrust.[2]

Given the intended audience of the *CEV*, story was determined to be more readily understood than "parable," and so it is consistently the preferred rendering, as in Mark 4.10, 11:

[2]Amos N. Wilder, *Jesus' Parables and the War of Myths* (Philadelphia: Fortress Press, 1982), p. 73.

When Jesus was alone with the twelve apostles and some others, they asked him about these *stories*. He answered:

I have explained the secret about God's kingdom to you, but can use only *stories*.

14. Red Sea

One of the most delicate issues was that of how to translate the Hebrew phrase *yam suph* traditionally rendered *Red Sea*. After much discussion over a period of several months and some sharing of correspondence, the decision was reached to continue with "Red Sea" in the text, and to follow each occurrence with one of several notes. The primary note is placed at Exodus 13.18:

> **Red Sea:** *Hebrew* yam suph *"Sea of Reeds," one of the marshes or fresh water lakes, near the eastern part of the Nile Delta. This identification is based on Exodus 13.17–14.9, which lists the towns on the route of the Israelites before crossing the sea. In the Greek translation of the Scriptures made about 200 B.C., the "Sea of Reeds" was named "Red Sea."*

At Exodus 23.31 the note is different:

> **Red Sea:** *Hebrew* yam suph, *here referring to the Gulf of Aqaba, since the term is extended to include the northeastern arm of the Red Sea (see also the note at 13.18).*

A similar note is included for the Gulf of Suez for Numbers 33.10, and in the New Testament for Acts 7.36 and Hebrews 11.29.

15. Virgin or Young Woman?

Beyond a doubt, the question of *virgin* or *young woman* for Isaiah 7.14 was the most sensitive issue in the entirety of the *CEV* project.

When translating any given biblical passage, three major considerations will always interact: (a) the evidence of biblical scholarship, (b) the perceived needs of the primary audience, whether church or non-church, and (c) the concerns of the church constituencies. What finally decided the issue in favor of "virgin" was the concern for "two thousand years of Christian tradition." So the verse was translated: "A virgin is pregnant; she will have a son and will name him Immanuel."

However, to help the reader understand the textual complexity behind this choice of words, a substantial note was added:

virgin: *Or "young woman." In this context the difficult Hebrew word did not imply a virgin birth. However, in the Greek translation made about 200 B.C. and used by the early Christians, the word* parthenos *had a double meaning. While the translator took it to mean "young woman," Matthew understood it to mean "virgin" and quoted the passage (Matthew 1.23) because it was the appropriate description of Mary, the mother of Jesus.*

16. Remain in My Love

In the entirety of the *CEV* project, the most difficult phrase to translate meaningfully proved to be "remain in my love" (John 15.9). In the Gospel of John, two words are sometimes used with the same meaning, as in "The Father loves (*agapao*) the Son" (3.35) and "The Father loves (*phileo*) the Son" (5.20). It is the **context** alone that tells us that the words each carry the same meaning, and it is the **context** that must serve as the clue for understanding the meaning of *agapao* ("love") in 15.9, 10. In the familiar John 3.16, this same verb is obviously used of God's *unconditional* love for everyone, whereas in John 15 "love" describes the unique relation between Jesus and his followers. This love is modeled after the love between the Father and Jesus, and it is set in the context of the story about the vine and its branches, which are "cut off and burned" if they don't "remain" in the vine (15. 6).

This seems to suggest that the "love" spoken of in John 15.9, 10 must be both *conditional* and *reciprocal*, and the nearest parallel in the other Gospels is found in Matthew 6.14, 15, where Jesus tells his followers, "If you forgive others for the wrongs they do to you, your Father in heaven will forgive you. But if you don't forgive others, *your Father will not forgive your sins.*" Neither John 15.9, 10 nor Matthew 6.14, 15 implies that God no longer "loves" or "forgives" the followers of Jesus, or that the gift of salvation is conditional. However, they do affirm that the unique bond (spoken of in John as "love") between Jesus and his followers can truly exist only when the followers are obedient and forgiving, in the same way that Jesus the Son is absolutely obedient to the Father and unconditionally forgiving of others. This is why the CEV translates "remain in my love" as "So remain faithful to my love for you."

Throughout the translation and review process the translators were concerned that the *CEV* would be a translation that people could understand whether they were members of faith communities or not, whether they had ever read the Bible before, or had never even gone to Sunday School. It was important to the translators that every word employed be one that any speaker of English could understand. Never was it assumed that every Bible reader would necessarily be familiar with traditional church language or with the phraseology found in traditional Bible translations. The message of the Bible is too important. It must be communicated clearly.

4
FINDING A PLACE:
HOW TO EVALUATE THE READABILITY
OF A BIBLE TRANSLATION

What Is "Readability"?

One of the questions frequently asked about the *Contemporary English Version* is, "What is its *reading level?*" Too often this question is based upon the false assumption that certain objective standards exist whereby a text can somehow be automatically "measured" or "weighed" to provide a precise answer. But this is not the case. In fact, the standards for readability testing are not flawless, and any conclusions can never be more than "probability statements." For example, if the *CEV* were evaluated to be grade 4, this would merely be saying that perhaps fifty to seventy percent of persons with a fourth grade education should have little or no difficulty reading it.

Most readability formulas focus on sentence length and vocabulary, though others include such factors as grammatical relationships and sentence structure. Unfortunately, these measurements tend to be *mechanical* and do not take into consideration the more subjective elements that are equally important. For example, a "short" sentence can be more difficult to comprehend than a "long" one, if the word order of the shorter one is unnatural and the longer one flows smoothly. Moreover, too many short, choppy sentences in sequence can actually have an adverse effect by diminishing the reader's interest. In this regard, compare the "interest level" of the two translations of Psalm 40.13-15 that were given the same "grade level" when evaluated by one standard test for readability (in the following examples, **B** represents the *CEV*):

A	**B**
Please, LORD, save me.	Please show that you care
Hurry, LORD, to save me.	and come to my rescue.
People are trying to kill me.	Hurry and help me!
Shame them and disgrace	
them.	Disappoint and confuse
People want to hurt me.	all who want me dead;
Let them run away in	turn away and disgrace
disgrace.	all who want to hurt me.
People are making fun of me.	Embarrass and shame
	all of those who say,
	"Just look at you now!"

Other than the series of choppy sentences in **A**, notice that five of the seven lines end in "me" and three of the seven begin with "people." Too much of this kind of repetition can contribute to loss of reader interest. The *CEV* (**B**) does not mention the LORD's name in this verse because the LORD has already been addressed by name in the immediately preceding verse.

A number of additional matters must be considered when attempting to determine the readability of a biblical text. One of particular importance concerns the shift in pronouns when speaking of the same individual (Psalm 99.2, 3). Both translations below were given the same grade level by a reading consultant, but the shift from *he* (third person pronoun) to *your* (second person pronoun) will cause severe misunderstanding for the reader of **A**:

A	**B**
The LORD in Jerusalem is great;	*You* are praised in Zion,
he is supreme over all the	and *you* control all nations
peoples.	Only *you* are God!
Let them praise *your* name;	And *your* power alone,
it is great, holy and to be	so great and fearsome,
feared.	is worthy of praise.

One of the classic examples of this confusing shift in pronominal references occurs in Song of Songs 1.2: "Let *him* kiss me with the kisses of *his* mouth! For *your* love is better than wine ..." Evidently such shifts signaled something important within the movement of Hebrew poetry, but the effect is lost on contemporary English readers.

Another factor that makes it difficult to evaluate Bible translations for their readability is that reviewers too easily overlook constructions that do not make sense, and don't really consider how stylistic details help to determine the readability of a text. For example, *because* is sometimes used to signal opposite meanings in the same context: "Take away the shame I fear, *because* your laws are good ... I have an answer for people who insult me, *because* I trust what you say" (Psalm 119.39,42); "All things continue to this day *because* of your laws, *because* all things serve you" (Psalm 119.91).

The texts that follow were taken from translations judged to have approximately the same comprehension level. Among other things, these verses are problematic in **A** because of an unsuccessful attempt to imitate the parallelism of the Hebrew text (see page 49 for an explanation of "parallelism").

A	B

Psalm 73.9

Their mouths lay claim to heaven,
   and their tongues take possession of
     the earth.

They dare to speak against God
   and to order others around.

Psalm 78.51

He struck down all the firstborn of Egypt,
   the firstfruits of manhood in the tents
     of Ham.

He killed the first-born son
   in every Egyptian family.

The Seven "Other" Readability Tests

To understand the many dimensions of what makes a text engaging, understandable, and readable, it might be worthwhile to consider the following readability tests. Each addresses issues that were constantly in the minds of the translators in their effort to make the *CEV* text as readable and understandable as possible.

1. Are the words and sentence patterns familiar?

Sentences should follow the informal patterns of everyday *spoken* English. This can be especially significant for people who have difficulty with standard English. In addition, educated readers have expressed appreciation for this feature because it gives a "conversational feeling" to the text. Sitting down to read the Bible can be like visiting with an old friend.

2. Are the thoughts easy to follow and understand?

No literature will stay long in a reader's hands if it is difficult to comprehend. Even faithful Bible readers complain because traditional translations are often so hard to understand. A young woman said to one of the *CEV* translators, "I am Polish, and I can understand the *CEV* better than I can my own Polish Bible that was translated in the sixties. Do you think it is right to make the Bible so easy to understand?" The answer is, "Not only is it right, it is our mission!" Many of the books which make up the Bible have a profound and complex character. Without diminishing that reality, if some of the passages in these books are not understood, the translators cannot claim to have done their work well.

3. Is it easy to read aloud?

This factor is discussed in more detail in chapter 8, "A New Approach to Bible Translation." But it should be emphasized here as well that the *CEV* is free of tongue-twisters. Each step of the way the translators have kept in mind that the *oral* readability of a text derives from giving careful attention to a number of stylistic details.

4. Is it easy to follow when read aloud?

Subconsciously, many readers at all levels occasionally "sound out" a text, especially if it displays lyrical qualities. One reader of the *CEV* — someone with a doctoral degree and a background in theater — suddenly noticed that, as he was reading the Gospel of John, he had unknowingly shifted from silent reading to oral reading, and found himself "listening" with great enjoyment. Another person said: "When I read the *CEV* to a congregation, they don't go 'Huh?', they say 'Hmm.'"

5. Is the text easy to follow on the page?

The *CEV* has attempted to create a text that is easy to look at, with a suitable amount of "white" space on the page. Not only does the *CEV* offer "measured lines" in poetry, but the lines are arranged as artistically as possible to enhance reading ease. And frequent paragraphing in prose sections keeps the text from being overwhelming, especially for unskilled readers. In a survey where high school and college students were asked to indicate what made books readable, at the top of the list were "short sentences and paragraphs."

Another unique feature of the *CEV* that assists readability is its use of block indentions for lengthy quotations such as parables and speeches. Setting the passage off in this manner makes it possible to eliminate the excessive use of double and single quotation marks which can clutter the page and make it difficult to tell who is speaking, and where exactly their speach begins and ends. In the *CEV* there is never more than one quotation within another.

6. Does it capture and hold your interest?

One reading specialist said, "*Readability is excitement.* A punchy beginning. Forceful and colorful language. Variety in style, including both long and short sentences." Without adding anything that is not part of the original language texts, the CEV translators have often been able to render the original meaning in an exciting and forceful manner.

7. Does it "sing to your heart and soul"?

"Soul appeal" — above all else — is a necessary ingredient for instilling readability into a translation of the Bible. This is an intrinsic feature that is easier *experienced* than explained. It is the "chemistry" that develops between the text and the reader, and it results from a detailed attention to all matters of literary style. During a denominational convention someone stopped by the ABS booth and was looking at the *CEV* New Testament with Psalms and Proverbs. The ABS representative asked, "Are you familiar with that publication?" She answered, "This is the first time I have seen one with Psalms and Proverbs. But I have read the New Testament, and it is clear and simple, like Christ intended; it just sings to your heart and soul!" A translation that "sings to your heart and soul" is one the reader will return to again and again.

Working for Clarity and Continuity in Prose

Even the most minute details are addressed in order to attain clarity and continuity in the prose sections of the *CEV*. Compare it (**B**) with a traditional rendering (**A**) of Luke 8.2, 3:

A	B
²... some women who had been cured of evil spirits and infirmities: Mary, called Magdalene, from whom seven demons had gone out, ³and Joanna, the wife of Herod's steward Chuza, and Susanna, and many others, who provided for them out of their resources.	²... some women who had been healed of evil spirits and all sorts of diseases. One of the women was Mary Magdalene, who once had seven demons in her. ³Joanna, Susanna, and many others had also used what they owned to help Jesus and his disciples. Joanna's husband Chuza was one of Herod's officials.

Unless the oral reader of **A** observes carefully how the descriptive phrases for both Mary Magdalene and Joanna have been structured, the hearer could easily assume that four women are indicated instead of three, the fourth being the unnamed wife of Herod's steward Chuza.

The *CEV* is also concerned with discourse continuity within larger sections of the biblical narrative such as Exodus 21–34, which is a lengthy series of instructions given by God to Moses and the people of Israel. At various intervals the Hebrew text indicates that God is the speaker, but these markers are inadequate for the modern reader who may be reading one section at a time and possibly at a point in the text where the speaker is not indicated. For example, one traditional translation introduces a new section heading at Exodus 23.14 as follows:

Three Annual Festivals

[14]"Three times a year you are to celebrate a festival to me. ..."

The section opens with a section heading, which is very useful, but the average reader won't have a clue why verse 14 begins with quotation marks, and there is no clear indication of who *me* refers to, since the last mention of the LORD as the speaker was several chapters earlier in Exodus 20.22.

The *CEV* translators have worked diligently to resolve these problems for the reader who may pick up the text and start reading at Exodus 23.14. As in the traditional translation, a new section heading is provided, but of more importance, the LORD is identified as the speaker by the use of words in italics, indicating that these words are not actually part of the Hebrew text, but were introduced as a device that is helpful to the reader:

Three Annual Festivals

The LORD said:
[14]Celebrate three festivals each year in my honor.

Notice also that in the *CEV*, quotation marks are not used in long speeches that extend for chapter after chapter — they serve no useful purpose and simply add clutter to the page. To make long speeches by a single speaker stand out on the page, the *CEV* translators have chosen to indent them as a block. With this device it is also easy to scan a page to see where a speech begins and ends.

For most of the prophetic books of the Old Testament, it seemed less confusing to the average reader if a first person form ("I") were used of the prophet, rather than the traditional third person form ("he"). To see the effects of this restructuring, compare the traditional rendering of Hosea 1.1, 3 (**A**) on the left with the *CEV* (**B**) on the right:

A	B
This is the message which the LORD gave Hosea son of Beeri during the time that Uzziah, Jotham, Ahaz and Hezekiah were kings of Judah, and Jeroboam son of Jehoash was king of Israel.	I am Hosea son of Beeri. When Uzziah, Jotham, Ahaz, and Hezekiah were the kings of Judah, and when Jeroboam son of Jehoash was king of Israel, the LORD spoke this message to me.

Hosea's Wife and Children

²When the LORD first spoke to Israel through Hosea, he said to Hosea, "Go and get married; your wife will be unfaithful, and your children will be just like her. In the same way my people have left me and become unfaithful."

³So Hosea married a woman named Gomer, the daughter of Diblaim. After the birth of their first child, a son ...

Hosea's Family

²The LORD said, "Hosea, Israel has betrayed me like an unfaithful wife. Marry such a woman and have children by her." ³So I married Gomer the daughter of Diblaim, and we had a son.

The opening verse reads with about equal ease in the two translations, though in **B** "this message" is tied more closely to what follows and is not interrupted by the mention of Hosea's father and of the kings of Israel and Judah. But in verses 2 and 3 (as shown in **B**) several significant improvements derive from the use of a first person reference to Hosea: (a) The difficult grammatical construction "he spoke to Israel *through* Hosea" is averted; (b) undue repetition is avoided ("spoke to Israel through *Hosea*, he said to *Hosea*), (c) a chronological order of events is achieved, as well as (d) an economy of style.

Small Matters Make a Big Difference

When it comes to the relationship between style and readability, small matters do indeed make a big difference. In translating, the paragraph should be considered the basic discourse unit, which means that within each paragraph, careful attention must be given to such matters as backgrounding and foregrounding, old and new information, focus, sequence and logical flow, implicit and explicit information, and transitional markers. In this light, compare the two translations of 2 Samuel 4.4:

A

Jonathan son of Saul had a son who was lame in both feet. He was five years old when the news about Saul and Jonathan came from Jezreel. His nurse picked him up and fled, but as she hurried to leave, he fell and became crippled. His name was Mephibosheth.

B

Saul's son Jonathan had a son named Mephibosheth, who had not been able to walk since he was five years old. It happened when someone from Jezreel told his nurse that Saul and Jonathan had died. She hurried off with the boy in her arms, but he fell and injured his legs.

Undue repetition — even of pronouns — can prove fatal to a reader's interest, as in the following translation of Luke 1.15-17, and can even result in pronominal ambiguity, as in the last clause (*he ... him*).

He will be a great man in the Lord's sight. *He* must not drink any wine or strong drink. From his very birth *he* will be filled with the Holy Spirit, and he will bring back many of the people of Israel to the Lord their God. *He* will go ahead of the Lord, strong and mighty, like the prophet Elijah. *He* will bring fathers and children together again; *he* will turn disobedient people back to the way of thinking of the righteous; *he* will get the Lord's people ready for *him.*

A similar example would be this translation of Mark 12.44: "But *she*, poor as *she* is, put in all *she* had — *she* gave all *she* had to live on." Here *she* is used five times within one relatively short sentence. The text is intelligible enough, but it does not "grab" a reader or "sing to the heart and soul."

To summarize, attention to details is at the heart of creating and crafting a readable text. The following are some of the rules that guided the *CEV* translators:

- use verbs instead of abstract nouns;
- introduce new ideas at proper intervals, and not too often;
- anticipate, rather than contradict, the reader's expectations;
- be alert to any shared information between the writer and the original recipients;
- use pronouns in ways that will be clear to the reader/hearer;
- vary sentence length to hold interest;
- use familiar patterns of ordinary speech;
- introduce characters and events in logical or chronological order;
- explain unfamiliar ideas in terms of familiar ones;
- avoid paragraphs that are too long or complicated;
- select forceful and colorful language;
- as much as the text being translated allows, open with punchy beginnings and close with powerful endings;
- guard against potentially ludicrous or misleading terms;
- listen to the sound of words and syllables;
- don't rely on silent punctuation marks to control intended oral emphases or pauses; and
- never use more than three unaccented syllables in a row.

A Seven-Point Checklist for a
Contemporary English Translation

❑ **Meaning**

A contemporary translation should be a faithful and systematic communication of meaning from one language to another.

❑ **Reading**

A contemporary translation should be one that the average person can read aloud without stumbling.

❑ **Hearing**

A contemporary translation should be one that can be heard without misunderstanding.

❑ **Feeling**

A contemporary translation considers the emotional impact of words.

❑ **Seeing**

In a contemporary translation, the appearance of the text on the page is important, because the format determines the ease by which the text can be read aloud and understood when heard. This is especially important in poetry.

❑ **Understanding**

A contemporary translation should be one that can be easily understood by the average reader or hearer, without the help of an interpreter.

❑ **Memorizing**

A contemporary translation uses economy of language, natural word order, and an appealing style to aid memorization.

5

UPHOLDING THE STANDARD:
A NEW LOOK AT ANCIENT POETRY

Respect for the Art of Poetry

As reading gives way to "viewing" in our culture, the reading of poetry has become virtually a thing of the past. Many people feel poetry is too difficult for them to understand without the aid of a professor or guide. Few ever willingly read it "on their own," or see it as something they could enjoy. Complaints include: "Poetry is full of obscure images that have to be figured out," "Poetry often alludes to things that are no longer a part of everyday life," and "Poetry sounds unnatural and uses strange word order." When poetry is translated from another language it can be even less appealing.

In the translation of biblical poetry, most traditional translations have had to sacrifice meter, rhyme, and other features that are significant when poetry is meant to be heard. But many of them have attempted to retain the *form* of the Hebrew without considering the need for creating an effective and appropriate English style. This is particularly evident in how the translations handle Hebrew parallelism, which appears frequently in Old Testament passages and which rarely carries over with equal effectiveness into English (see page 49).

Poetry with Impact and Power

No translation is perfect; all translation involves difficult choices and repeated efforts to find the best wording. Below are seven ways in which the *CEV* has attempted to deal creatively with poetic passages in the Bible, and to bring out their power and impact in English. Psalm 18, which is printed out in full on p. 90ff., serves as the primary point of reference.

1. Measured lines

The choice of line breaks in poetry is no less integral to the translation than is the choice of words, and to alter the lines may result in a *mistranslation*, especially for the *hearer*. Keep in mind that more people *hear* the Bible read than read it for themselves. For this reason, the translators of the *CEV* decided where each line would break, rather than leaving that decision to either the typesetter or the computer. The *CEV* line breaks are not always ideal, because the line length in most double-column format Bibles is very limiting. But it has been possible to exercise some control as to where the breaks occurred without creating unnecessary confusion.

2. Addressing God directly

In liturgical, confessional, and poetic passages, Hebrew frequently shifts between second person ("you") and third person ("he") references to God. For English speakers it is generally more natural to employ only a second person pronoun ("you"), because the shifting back and forth between "you" and "he" is often confusing.

Where shifts are made in longer sections, and where the biblical writer is obviously changing from addressing God directly to making an open declaration about God, the shifts are honored in the *CEV*. But in a psalm such as 18, these shifts often frustrate English speakers who are more comfortable with a consistent form of address. And so, in this particular psalm the *CEV* uses a second person ("you") reference throughout.

3. Economy of words and poetic form

In the *CEV*, Psalm 18 consists of 173 lines, making it 25 lines shorter than one traditional translation and 17 lines shorter than another. The *CEV* still employs a traditional style, consisting of alternating primary and secondary lines. But it has also introduced a different form — in which two primary lines are followed by one secondary line. Psalm 18.11:

> Darkness was your robe;
> thunderclouds filled the sky,
> > hiding you from sight.

The result is a wider variety of format, no runover lines, and, quite often, fewer lines overall in a poetic section without any loss of content. Most importantly, these factors contribute significantly toward achieving an ease of oral reading without stumbling and of hearing without misunderstanding. Taken together, these factors aid memorization.

4. The paragraph as the basic translation unit

In translation, the basic unit of concern is the paragraph, because all sentences within a paragraph must somehow be connected, and the relation of the paragraph to what precedes and what follows must be connected. In the Hebrew Psalms, God is often addressed more frequently within a paragraph than might sound natural in English. For this reason, in the *CEV* one noun of address is sometimes pushed forward to the beginning of a paragraph, while others within the paragraph may not need to be repeated explicitly. Occasionally, two nouns of address (for example, "LORD" and "God") that occur on separate lines (or in separate verses) of the Hebrew text are brought together near the beginning of the paragraph, as in verses 1, 2 of Psalm 18:

> ¹I love you, *LORD God,*
>> and you make me strong.
> ² You are my mighty rock,
>> my fortress, my protector,
> the rock where I am safe...

Compare this with the following traditional translation, which retains the form of the Hebrew text.

> ¹ I love you, *O LORD*, my strength.
> ² *The LORD* is my rock, my
>> fortress and my deliverer,
> *my God*, my rock in whom I
>> take refuge...

5. Abbreviated and embedded nouns of address

Unfortunately, the forms "O LORD" and "O God," as well as "my LORD" and "my God," especially when occurring in the initial position in a sentence, may sound to some like a form of swearing, and so these expressions have usually been avoided in *CEV* poetry. In fact, the translators have often embedded the nouns of address for the deity, altering the word order, as in Psalm 18.1, 3, 20, 28, 30, and 49. A notable exception is found in Psalm 22.1, where the traditional wording has been retained: "My God, my God, why have you deserted me?"

6. Parallelism

Parallelism is a primary feature of Hebrew poetry, where it is far more common than in the English literary tradition. It occurs in many different and complex forms, the most common of which is synonymous parallelism, where successive lines repeat the same theme using different words. Some examples from traditional translations are:

Psalm 43.5

> Why are you cast down, O my soul,
>> and why are you disquieted within me?

Psalm 103.10

> He does not deal with us according to our sins,
>> nor repay us according to our iniquities

For persons unfamiliar with the biblical literary tradition, the use of parallelism in English may at times sound cumbersome and awkward if used too frequently. Parallelism does exist in *CEV* poetry, but to a lesser degree and in a different format than in traditional translations, for example:

Psalm 18.4,5

Death had wrapped
    its ropes around me,
and I was almost swallowed
    by its flooding waters.

Ropes from the world
of the dead
    had coiled around me,
and death had set a trap
    in my path.

7. Textual visualization

For the most part, the style of the *CEV* poetry is significantly different from that of other translations, because the translators are concerned with matters of *textual visualization* and *aesthetics*. It is expected of poetry, not only that it *sound* good, but that it *look* good when it is laid out on the page. The discussion at the end of this chapter explains how this was achieved in Psalm 8 using a single-column format. Compare this with the equally readable double-column format demonstrated in the examples given in Appendix B under the heading "Beautiful Poetry That's Easy To Follow", p. 88 ff.

Poetry Is Pleasant To Experience

In the translation of poetry, at least the following factors must be considered: form, rhythm, rhyme, sound, imagery, sensitivity, and memorization. The *CEV* translators were constantly aware of these concerns, as can be demonstrated by calling attention to seven features of *CEV* poetry:

1. Simple and straightforward

There is a significant difference between a text that is simple and one that is simplistic. The former deals with complex issues in an unpretentious and pleasing manner; the latter ignores complex issues. The former is concerned with matters of style; the latter disregards stylistic details and is often laboriously literal, as in Psalm 65.12,13:

Traditional	***CEV***
The grasslands of the desert overflow;	Desert pastures blossom,
the hills are clothed with gladness.	and mountains celebrate.
The meadows are covered with flocks	Meadows are filled
and the valleys are mantled with	with sheep and goats;
grain;	valleys overflow with grain
they shout for joy and sing.	and echo with joyful songs.

A second feature of CEV poetry is its concern for the sounds of letters, syllables, words, and phrases, as may be seen in Habakkuk 3.17,18:

2. Sound

Traditional	**CEV**
Though the fig tree does not bud	Fig trees may no longer bloom,
and there are no grapes on the vines,	or vineyards produce grapes;
though the olive crop fails	olive trees may be fruitless,
and the fields produce no food,	and harvest time a failure;
though there are no sheep in the pen	sheep pens may be empty,
and no cattle in the stalls,	and cattle stalls vacant —
yet I will rejoice in the LORD,	but I will still celebrate
I will be joyful in God my Savior.	because the LORD God
	saves me.

Among other things, notice how the traditional translation unnecessarily repeats *the* ("the fig tree . . . the vines . . . the olive crop . . . the fields . . . the pen . . . the stalls") and retains traditional biblical phrases such as "rejoice in the Lord" and "be joyful in God." On the other hand, every detail of the *CEV* has been crafted to create an appealing sequence of sounds. In crafting the *CEV* poetry, the translators carefully went over each line again and again to be sure each would be easy to read aloud and pleasant to hear. Distracting rhyming schemes and singsong rhythms were avoided. (See the discussion on p. 77 for more detail on how this is accomplished.)

3. Sequence

As much as possible, the *CEV* attempts to restructure the elements of each thought unit — even in poetry — so that a logical and/or chronological sequence is accomplished. Isaiah 33.15,16 is a good example:

Traditional	**CEV**

He who walks righteously
  and speaks what is right,
who rejects gain from extortion
  and keeps his hand from accepting
    bribes,
who stops his ears against plots of
    murder
  and shuts his eyes against
    contemplating evil —
this is the man who will dwell on the
    heights,
  whose refuge will be the mountain
    fortress.
His bread will be supplied,
  and water will not fail him.
	But there will be rewards
	  for those who live right
	    and tell the truth,
	for those who refuse
	    to take money by force
	    or accept bribes,
	for all who hate murder
	    and violent crimes.
	They will live in a fortress
	  high on a rocky cliff,
	where they will have food
	  and plenty of water.

By mentioning the matter of "rewards" at the very first, the *CEV* "sets the stage" for all that follows, whereas the reader of the traditional text will have to retain in mind everything from the beginning of the text down to "contemplating evil" before understanding the significance of "He who ... who ... who ... this is the man who."

4. Succinctness

In the translation of poetry, *every* word is significant. And each contributes to the reader's understanding of the text. Observe two passages from Job in this regard:

Traditional	**CEV**

Job 38.34, 35

Can you raise your voice to the
    clouds
  and cover yourself with a flood of
    water?
Do you send the lightning bolts on
    their way?
  Do they report to you, 'Here we are?'
	Can you order the clouds
	    to send a downpour,
	or will lightning flash
	    at your command?

Job 41.15-17

His back has rows of shields
   tightly sealed together;
each is so close to the next
   that no air can pass between.
They are joined fast to one another;
   they cling together and cannot be
    parted.

Its back is covered
   with shield after shield,
firmly bound and closer together
   than breath to breath.

5. Sensitivity

In poetry, as well as in prose, the *CEV* is a translation that has been sensitively and diligently refined to bring out the imagery and impact in poetry, as may be illustrated by an example from Job. One motto of the *CEV* is: "In translating poetry, imagery and impact are more important than pedantic precision." What this means can be quickly demonstrated by examining two translations, descriptions of a crocodile found in Job:

A   **B**

Job 41.30

The scales on his belly are like
   jagged pieces of pottery;
   they tear up the muddy ground
   like a threshing sledge.

As it crawls through the mud,
its sharp and spiny hide
   tears the ground apart.

In **A** an unsuccessful attempt was made to transfer the literal imagery of the Hebrew poetry over into English, and the result is a text that is (a) jingly ("belly ... pottery ... muddy"), (b) unappealing in its imagery ("jagged pieces of pottery ... threshing sledge"), and (c) difficult to follow (because line breaks separate adjectives from the nouns they modify). On the other hand, **B** has tried to create the picture of a crocodile slowly crawling through mud — the rhythm is appropriate, and the imagery and impact accurately convey the intent of the Hebrew text.

6. Sense

"Sense versus nonsense" is a constant struggle in the translation of biblical poetry, and translators must constantly endeavor to achieve both accuracy and clarity, as in Psalm 147.10, or again in Proverbs 30.20, where the reader of some traditional translations is left frustrated and confused because the text seems to focus on "table manners," but the writer of Proverbs is actually concerned about a person taking unfaithfulness no more seriously than eating.

Traditional	**CEV**

Psalm 147.10

His pleasure is not in the strength of the horse, nor his delight in the legs of a man.	The LORD doesn't care about the strength of horses or powerful armies.

Proverbs 30.20

This is the way of an adulteress: She eats and wipes her mouth and says, 'I've done nothing wrong.'	An unfaithful wife says, "Sleeping with another man is as natural as eating."

7. Shape

Textual visualization and measured lines are basic components of *CEV* poetry. Compare the "shape of things" in the two following translations of Psalm 8.1, 2 as they actually appear in published editions:

Traditional	**CEV**
O LORD, our Sovereign, how majestic is your name in all the earth! You have set your glory above the heavens. Out of the mouths of babes and infants you have founded a bulwark because of your foes, to silence the enemy and the avenger.	Our LORD and Ruler, your name is wonderful everywhere on earth! You let your glory be seen in the heavens above. With praises from children and from tiny infants, you have built a fortress. It makes your enemies silent, and all who turn against you are left speechless.

More about how the translators made important decisions in laying out the text on the page may be found in chapter 4, especially p. 41.

A Pleasing Alternative

Not only has the *CEV* poetry been designed to accommodate the double-column format of most Bibles, but it has also been set in a single-column format, for publications where this is either necessary or preferable, as may be seen for Psalm 8:

The Wonderful Name of the LORD

¹Our LORD and Ruler,
    your name is wonderful everywhere on earth!
You let your glory be seen in the heavens above.
²With praises from children and from tiny infants,
    you have built a fortress.
It makes your enemies silent,
    and all who turn against you are left speechless.

³I often think of the heavens your hands have made,
    and of the moon and stars you put in place.
⁴Then I ask, "Why do you care about us humans?
    Why are you concerned for us weaklings?"
⁵You made us a little lower than you yourself,
    and you have crowned us with glory and honor.

⁶You let us rule everything your hands have made.
And you put all of it under our power —
⁷   the sheep and the cattle, and every wild animal,
⁸   the birds in the sky, the fish in the sea,
    and all ocean creatures.

⁹Our LORD and Ruler,
    your name is wonderful everywhere on earth!

Poetry makes up almost one fifth of the Bible's literature and includes some of the most powerful expressions of respect and love for the Creator. The translators of the *CEV* have taken great care to see that the meaning of this poetry is communicated in a way that is both clear and a lively and inspiring experience.

6

TAKING ON SENSITIVE ISSUES: CAREFUL CONSIDERATION OF CULTURAL CONCERNS

The translators of the *CEV* have worked hard to make the *Contemporary English Version* a translation that everyone who uses English can accept and use joyfully, whether alone or in groups. It is a translation that has the normal flow and rhythms of modern English speech and that remains true to the historical and cultural contexts in which that message was received. To be faithful to the universal nature of the Bible's appeal, the translators took special care that the *CEV* did not needlessly alienate women or Jews by ignoring the original contexts of the passages being translated.

Guidelines for Gender Generic Language

In order to be sensitive to the need for gender generic language, sometimes called inclusive language, a number of guidelines were established at the beginning of the *CEV* project by the Translations Subcommittee of the American Bible Society. These include:

(1) In all passages involving gender generic language, a primary concern will be to create a *style* that is natural and appropriate for the intended audience.

(2) Where the source language uses masculine nouns or pronouns in a generic sense, the translation will reflect this intent by using gender generic equivalents in modern English.

(3) No attempt will be made to disguise the gender of specific individuals.

(4) Although there is an awareness of and a vital concern for the sensitivities of the readers, the historical, cultural, and sociological setting of the *biblical* text must be accurately reflected in the translation at all times, even when this contradicts modern understandings of masculine and feminine roles.

(5) An attempt will be made to render all pronominal references to persons (whether male or female) as unobtrusively as possible and to substitute nouns wherever the flow of the discourse allows.

Applying the Guidelines for Gender Generic Language

It is one thing to establish a set of guidelines for the use of gender generic language, but it is an entirely different matter to *apply* these principles with sound judgment. So in this section some of these principles will be further elaborated and examples given for their application in specific contexts.

Gender Generic but Culture Specific

God is neither masculine nor feminine. And God is certainly not neuter, or impersonal. God is *God,* and as such is beyond all categories of gender. But Bible translators must deal with the *particularity* of history — in this case the historical setting of the biblical writings.

The many male metaphors for deity found in the Bible reflect backgrounds in a patriarchal society. Although recent scholarly studies have called attention to the use of female imagery for God in the Bible, it is still the masculine terms, such as Father, Lord, and Son, which are most frequently used. For translators to deny this patriarchal context by altering such terms would be to misrepresent history.

It should be noted that there is a basic difference between *translation* and *transculturation.* A translation must reflect the particularity of the original historical cultural setting. And one may no more remove from the Bible the metaphor of God as Father than one may transfer the imagery of Jesus as "Lamb of God" to that of "Pig of God" for the Iban tribes of Borneo, where pigs are the most prized animals, as transculturation might suggest. Similarly, many peoples of Southeast Asia have what anthropologists term a rice culture. But to shift from "bread" to "rice" in Bible translation would destroy the historical integrity and setting of the biblical message.

The metaphor of God as Father is as essential to the core of the Bible as were the "Goddess of Heaven" and "Mother Earth" in other ancient civilizations. Remove this metaphor, and the Bible is immediately uprooted from its cultural heritage. A contemporary example is found among certain Dani tribes of Irian Jaya, Indonesia, where — contrary to most cultures — the sun is regarded as feminine and the moon as masculine. In translating Dani oral traditions into English, these distinctions *must* be retained; otherwise, the translation is inaccurate.

From a purely linguistic viewpoint, the problem is only slightly less complicated. For example, the words "God" and "Lord" are masculine in English only because they have feminine counterparts. Otherwise, English nouns do not have grammatical gender or require masculine pronouns. Moreover, alternative terms such as "Creator" lack the emotive value of "Father." Even in situations where a "Father" figure may have certain negative connotations, the term still represents an identifiable, personal being, whereas "Creator" may signal an impersonal, unidentifiable entity of some sort.

In American English "my mother" or "my father" might be used by a child, but never "my parent." One translation of the Gospel of John has Jesus addressing God as "my heavenly Parent" — a usage which could possibly mislead the reader in several ways.

So in the *CEV* the imagery of God as "Father" has been retained. However, it must be realized that even in the "Father" imagery of biblical texts, the focus is *not* upon God's *gender*, but rather upon God's attributes as one who supremely loves all people, regardless of their gender, age, race, or social status.

The situation is significantly different where the biblical languages use masculine forms when referring to groups of people of mixed gender. In this respect, guideline 2 is relevant: "Where the source language uses masculine nouns or pronouns in a generic sense, the translation will reflect this intent by using gender generic equivalents in modern English." The *basic* reason that biblical languages use masculine nouns of mixed groups is because these languages force the writer or speaker to choose between masculine and feminine forms when referring to people in general. For example, when the *King James Version* uses "children of Israel," it actually translates a masculine form in Hebrew ("sons of Israel"). Hebrew has a word for "son" and a word for "daughter," but none for "children" — and so for groups of mixed gender the masculine form is used. In English it is possible to say "they" without signaling gender; in Hebrew and Greek the speaker is obligated to say either "they (female)" or "they (male)." But to retain that kind of gender distinction in English, when the biblical writer intends both sexes, is a misrepresentation of the intent of the biblical text. Whenever it was clear from the context and grammar that both men and women were considered to be part of a group being discussed, the translators of the *CEV* have followed this principle: in such cases it would misrepresent the intent of the original text to limit its application to men only. An example would be Luke 5.10, where *CEV* translates "From now on you will bring in people instead of fish."

Inclusive but Unobtrusive

Whereas the preceding discussion concerned the *particularity* of history, this discussion concerns the *peculiarity* of language — in this case the English language. A primary concern of the *CEV* translators in their effort to create a gender generic text was that of naturalness — gender generic language should not call attention to itself. Readers of the *CEV* will never encounter the phrase "his or her." Nor will they see laborious and painful sentences such as the one found in one translation's rendering of Numbers 35.26, 27, where "slayer" and "avenger" represent attempts to be gender generic:

> But if the *slayer* shall at any time go outside the bounds of the original city
> of refuge, and is found by the *avenger* of blood outside the bounds of the
> city of refuge, and is killed by the *avenger*, no bloodguilt shall be incurred.

By shifting to a second person form ("you"), or by taking advantage of certain other translation techniques (see the following paragraphs), the *CEV* is able to achieve a more appropriate level of style. Note, however, that a masculine pronoun ("he") is retained for the "avenger of blood," since this person was assumed to be a male relative in the biblical culture (see guideline 4 on p. 56):

> But if you ever leave the Safe Town and are killed by the victim's relative,
> he cannot be punished for killing you.

An example of another approach to maintaining the gender generic intention of the original text is found in Romans 12.20. Where "your enemy" is used four consecutive times by one "inclusive language" translation (**A**) in order to keep from using a masculine pronoun, the *CEV* (in a poetry format) shifts to a plural because "your enemy" functions here as a plural (**B**). The result is simpler and more effective:

A	**B**
If *your enemy* is hungry, feed *your enemy*,	If *your enemies* are hungry,
if *your enemy* is thirsty, give *your enemy*	give *them* something to eat.
something to drink.	And if *they* are thirsty,
	give *them* something
	to drink.

Creating a Gender Generic Text

Gender generic language in the *CEV* was created in several different ways, among them: (1) by shifting from a singular *(him)* to a plural *(them,* as in Romans 12.20 above), or (2) by using *people* instead of *man (men)*, or (3) by shifting from a third person masculine singular pronoun *(he)* to a second person pronoun *(you)*.

However, before discussing these three techniques, it will be valuable to examine Micah 7.18-20, where the repeated shifting in Hebrew from a second person reference to God ("you") to a third person reference ("he") is problematic both for the reader and the hearer. Understanding how consistency can aid reader comprehension, the *CEV* translators adopted a pattern more suitable for its target audience (guideline #1, p. 56) by shifting to a *you* form throughout (column **B**):

A	**B**
Who is a God like you, pardoning iniquity and passing over the transgression of the remnant of your possession? He does not retain his anger forever, because he delights in showing clemency. He will again have compassion upon us; he will tread our iniquities under foot. You will cast all our sins into the depths of the sea. You will show faithfulness to Jacob and unswerving loyalty to Abraham, as you have sworn to our ancestors from the days of old.	Our God, no one is like you. We are all that is left of your chosen people, and you freely forgive our sin and guilt. You don't stay angry forever; you're glad to have pity and pleased to be merciful. You will trample on our sins and throw them in the sea. You will keep your word and be faithful to Jacob and to Abraham, as you promised our ancestors many years ago.

1. Shifting from singular to plural

In an attempt to be inclusive, one traditional translation of Matthew 16.27 loses the focus of the text, because "he will reward everyone for what has been done" is overly general and does not imply personal responsibility.

The *CEV* uses "all *people* for what *they* have done," though "*everyone* for what *they* have done" would also have been acceptable.

The well-known maxim that "a prophet is not honored in his own hometown" may also be shifted to a plural form: "Prophets are not honored in their own hometown."

2. Using "people" instead of "man" or "men"

A prime example of this technique is found in Psalm 1.1, 2, where *people* substitutes for *man*, which in turn is followed by the generic pronouns *they* and *them*:

> God blesses those people
>> who refuse evil advice
>> and won't follow sinners
>> or join in sneering God.
> Instead, the Law of the Lord
>> makes them happy,
>> and they think about it
>> day and night.

In Matthew 9.8 *people* is used instead of *men* — "... and praised God for giving such authority to *people*."

3. Changing from "he" to "you"

The Greek of Matthew 16.24 is literally, "If anyone wants to follow me, *he* must deny *himself* and take up *his* cross and follow me." The *CEV* shifts to a form which is still accurate, and at the same time more natural and effective in English: "If any of *you* want to be my followers, *you* must forget about *yourself*. *You* must take up *your* cross and follow me."

One traditional translation has handled this same verse by shifting to a third person plural form: "If any want to become my followers, let *them* deny *themselves* and take up *their* cross and follow me." Although this is possible, the expression "take up their cross" seems somewhat ambiguous, possibly implying collective possession of a single cross.

4. Using alternative noun forms

In addition to the three techniques discussed above, there are other ways of making the language generic. One such technique was used in Matthew 13.31,45, 46. The traditional translation (**A**), in its attempt to be generic, made only half of the journey ("someone ... his" and "a merchant ... he ... he"). It should be noted that guideline #5 on p. 57 ("to substitute nouns wherever the flow of the discourse allows") is applied in **B** by the *CEV* ("shop owner ... the owner").

A	B
(a) The kingdom of heaven is like a mustard seed that *someone* took and sowed in *his* field.	(a) The kingdom of heaven is like what happens when a *farmer* plants a mustard seed in *a* field.
(b) Again, the kingdom of heaven is like a *merchant* in search of fine pearls; on finding one pearl of great value, he went and sold all that *he* had and bought it.	(b) The kingdom of heaven is like what happens when a *shop owner* is looking for fine pearls. After finding a very valuable one, *the owner* goes and sells everything in order to buy that pearl.

5. Substituting passive verb constructions

Shifting from a subject followed by an active verb ("the men did so and so") to a passive verb with an implied subject ("so and so was done") is another way of creating gender generic language. However, this is the technique which the *CEV* translators have viewed as least helpful. Any text which relies heavily on passive verbs is usually flat and unexciting. It can also create ambiguity by making the reader uncertain about who is responsible for the actions being described. A look at one traditional translation's rendering of Matthew 13.47 will show what can happen:

> Again, the kingdom of heaven is like a net that was thrown into the sea and caught *fish* of every kind; when it was full, *they* drew it ashore, sat down, and put the good into baskets but threw out the bad.

The problem is that "*they* drew it ashore" must refer back grammatically to "*fish* of every kind," since no other subject is previously mentioned in the verse. In Greek, *they* (of "they drew it ashore") is literally "*men* drew it ashore." This reflects the biblical culture in which men seem to have done the commercial fishing, and it deals with a specific incident (see guideline #4, p. 56), which is the basis for the retention of the masculine reference ("fishermen") in the *CEV* — ". . . it is dragged to the shore, and the *fishermen* sit down to separate the fish . . ."

"The Jews" (οἱ Ἰουδαῖοι)

As with gender generic language, the *CEV* endeavors to be as sensitive as possible when translating the Greek phrase *the* Jews (οἱ Ἰουδαῖοι), which occurs most frequently in John and Acts. As demonstrated in the discussion of gender generic language, the key concern of the translators was to analyze carefully the intent of the original writers of the Scriptures each time this phrase is used, and then to provide the most appropriate rendering based on the context in which it occurs. The Mediterranean world of the first century A.D. was ethnically and religiously diverse. The Jewish population of Judea, and its capital Jerusalem, was made up of diverse movements, communities, factions, and interest groups. Since the previous century, real civil authority in Judea was exercised by Rome and its appointed governors. Roman civil authorities, however, did allow the Jewish people some independence in religious matters. The writers of the New Testament clearly understood the complexities of this arrangement. Although the New Testament has come to be understood as the primary document of the early Christian Church, it is important to remember that Jesus, his disciples, and all of the earliest "believers in Jesus as Messiah" were Jews.

Yet the frequent appearance in the New Testament of the apparently collective phrase *the Jews* in negative contexts has led some readers to wrongly conclude that the Christian Scriptures speak only of two categories of people — Christians and Jews, the one group appearing to be good, and the other not. Such a reading, however, is ultimately misleading.

In most of the New Testament the phrase *the Jews* is best understood to mean "the other Jews," "some of the Jews," "a few of the Jews" or "a Jewish group," "the Jewish leaders," "some of the Jewish leaders" or "a few of the Jewish leaders." Never does it refer to the entire Jewish people as a whole.

There are at least two ways in which the *CEV* has been carefully crafted to produce a New Testament text that is both *faithful* to its original social context and stylistically appropriate.

1. Making it clear where only some Jews are intended

Obviously "the Jews" *cannot* in *any* of the Gospels be *inclusive* of the entirety of the Jewish people, since the followers of Jesus were themselves Jews. It is the responsibility of the translators to make meaning clear, and so it is their task to determine precisely who is intended in any given passage. Sometimes this task is easy; sometimes it is difficult. What follows is a sampling from the Gospel of John where the Greek phrase "the Jews" is represented in English by a term that is less broadly inclusive (and thus more clear for the modern reader) in regard to the first century Jewish context. In verses where "the people" occurs in the *CEV*, it was felt that the context clearly implies that these are *Jewish* people. In other contexts "Jewish" seemed a necessary modifier.

(a) John 1.19, 20: "The *leaders* in Jerusalem sent priests and temple helpers ..."

(b) John 2.18: "The *Jewish leaders* asked Jesus ..."

(c) John 7.35: "The *people* asked each other ..."

(d) John 11.54: "Stopped going around *in public*" (= "openly among the Jews")

(e) John 18.12: "The Roman officer ... together with the *temple police*" (= "the Jewish officials")

(f) John 18.20: "... the temple, where all of our *people* come together."

(g) John 18.31: "The *crowd* replied ..."

(h) John 18.36: "... would have fought to keep me from being handed over to our *leaders* ..."

2. Relying on clear narrative flow

Because the *CEV* structures narrative passages in ways that are natural to modern English speech, another way to deal faithfully and naturally with this concern is at the level of the complete narrative, where persons are first identified fully, then in lesser degree (often only by pronouns) throughout the remainder of the discourse.   For example, in Galatians 2.13 the *CEV* has simply "the others" where the Greek reads "the other *Jews*," because the reference is clearly identified by the "Jewish followers" mentioned in verse 12 (see 73 ff., "Problems with Pronouns"). Once again, a few passages from the Gospel of John will help clarify how this is accomplished:

(a) John 5.10,15,16,18: "... the *Jewish leaders* saw the man ... [he] told the *leaders* ... *They* started making a lot of trouble for Jesus ... the *leaders* wanted to kill Jesus..."

(b) John 6.4,41,52: "... time for the *Jewish* festival ... The *people* started grumbling ... *They* started arguing ..."

(c) John 9.18,22 (twice): "... the *Jewish leaders* would not believe ... afraid of their *leaders*. The *leaders* had already agreed..."

The Bible is truly God's word for everyone, and the translators of the *CEV* felt a special burden to see that no one should feel excluded from its important message through a careless disregard for the cultural context in which the original documents were produced. Guiding them through this challenge was Paul's bold statement, "Faith in Christ Jesus is what makes each of you equal with each other, whether you are a Jew or a Greek, a slave or a free person, a man or a woman. So if you belong to Christ, you are now part of Abraham's family, and you will be given what God has promised." (Galatians 3.28, 29.)

7

HELPING THE READER:
WHAT BESIDES THE TEXT MAKES A BIBLE
EASY TO READ AND ENJOY?

Research into biblical illiteracy shows that resistance to reading the Bible is due, not only to an inability to understand the text, but to an inability to comprehend the cultural and historical context of the biblical narratives. The translators of the *CEV* realized that helps would be needed to "bridge the gap" between the Bible text and the contemporary reader. Here are examples of some special features that can be found in most editions of *CEV* Bibles and New Testaments.

Informative Introductions

An overall preface to the *Contemporary English Version* briefly informs the reader of the principles and procedures adopted for this translation of the Bible.

A brief introduction to each of the two Testaments indicates the various groupings of the books. For example, the Old Testament introduction begins as follows:

> The Old Testament is a collection of 39 books written in Hebrew, with a few chapters written in Aramaic. These books are arranged in five groups in English Bibles:
>
> (1) *The Pentateuch*. The name means "five books," and this group is made up of Genesis, Exodus, Leviticus, Numbers, and Deuteronomy. The group is sometimes called the "Law of Moses" or the "Torah," a Hebrew word referring to God's "law" or "teachings"...

In addition, each book of the Bible is introduced briefly. These introductions emphasize their major theme or themes, and are accompanied by a general outline of the book. Without inserting doctrinal note or comment, these introductions quickly orient the reader to the book which follows and provide a brief overview that the reader can refer back to frequently. The introduction (entitled "About this Letter") to Philippians begins:

Paul wrote this letter from jail (1.7) to thank the Lord's followers at Philippi for helping him with their gifts and prayers (1.5; 4.10-19). He hopes to be set free, so that he can continue preaching the good news (3.17-19). But he knows that he might be put to death (1.21; 2.17; 3.10).

Clearly Marked Sections

The chapter and verse markings that modern readers of the Bible often take for granted are really rather recent inventions in the history of the copying and publication of Bibles. Many Bible readers are surprised to learn that the original authors of the biblical books did not indicate chapter and verse divisions in their writings. In fact, chapter divisions were first developed for the Latin Vulgate in A.D. 1204 by the Archbishop of Canterbury, Stephen Langton. Verse division was first introduced into the Greek New Testament by Robert Stephanus in A.D. 1551, and the first English Bible to adopt verse markings was the Geneva Bible of A.D. 1560.

Although the *CEV* retains much of this traditional way of marking the text of the Bible, so that readers will be able to compare other translations with ease and to use the many helpful Bible commentaries and reference works available, it has also broken the text down into topical units or sections. Each of these sections is clearly marked by a descriptive heading. Some of these, especially in the New Testament Gospels, include references to passages with similar or parallel content. This allows readers to quickly find and compare multiple accounts of the same event or narrative. Additional cross references, such as to passages where the biblical author quotes or alludes to a biblical passage or event, are provided in the footnotes.

Helpful Notes

The *CEV* employs a number of different kinds of notes to help readers understand the biblical text. These clarify important matters without imposing a particular theological or doctrinal viewpoint.

1. Textual notes

As difficult as it may be for some Bible readers to accept, there are some parts of the Bible text that have proved almost impossible to translate. This is often because a certain word, phrase or idiom may occur only once in the entire Bible, and it has no supporting examples from any known secular or religious writings from the same period of history. Where these difficulties occur, translators still make their best efforts to render them into modern language, but are quick to point out their concern in a footnote. Many traditional translators say either "Hebrew unclear" or "meaning of Hebrew uncertain." Whenever it is possible, the *CEV* translators prefer to indicate other possible renderings in the footnote. In the *CEV* the text of Romans 8.28 has "God is always at work for the good of everyone who loves him," and the note gives two alternative possibilities: "Or, 'All things work for the good of everyone who loves God' or 'God's Spirit always works for the good of everyone who loves God.'"

In some cases the text is so difficult that there are no clear alternatives. In these instances the *CEV* tries to be as positive as possible. One example is Proverbs 26.10, which is perhaps the most obscure verse in the entire book of Proverbs. The *CEV* translates "It's no smarter to shoot arrows at every passerby, than it is to hire a bunch of worthless nobodies." This is followed with a footnote,

> **nobodies:** *One possible meaning for the difficult Hebrew text of verse 10.*

2. Historical notes

There are numerous historical notes in the *CEV*. In Haggai 1.1 the text reads "On the first day of the sixth month of the second year that Darius was king of Persia,* the LORD told Haggai the prophet to speak his message to the governor of Judea and to the high priest." A note accompanies the translation:

> 1.1 **sixth month ... king of Persia:** *Elul, the sixth month of the Hebrew calendar, from about mid-August to mid-September; the second year of the rule of Darius was 520 B.C.*

These kinds of notes help the readers quickly understand the historical and seasonal context of the narrative they are reading.

3. Cultural notes

Cultural notes are used to explain social, religious, or cultural events and realities that may be important for understanding the text, but cannot be included in the body of the translation. Genesis 38.8 reads: "It's your duty to marry Tamar and have a child for your brother." The significance of this remark is explained in a note: "If a man died without having children, his brother was to marry the dead man's wife and have a child, who was to be considered the child of the dead brother (see Deuteronomy 25.5)."

Perhaps the most frequently occurring cultural note found in the *CEV* is the one which explains the term "mighty rock." It reads:

> **mighty rock:** *The Hebrew text has "rock," which is sometimes used in poetry to compare the Lord to a mountain where his people can run for protection from their enemies.*

4. Notes to Explain Plays on Words

One of the unfortunate realities of translation from one language to another is the loss of relationships between words that is based on the way they sound. Because these puns tend to lose their punch when translated, a footnote is often required to point out to the reader the connections that were being suggested in the original language. This kind of note is often necessary in the Old Testament where the names of persons and places frequently relate to some significant event or characteristic.

An example of a passage where a footnote adds significantly to the understanding of the text is Jeremiah 1.11, 12, which relates a dialogue between God and the prophet.

> The LORD showed me something in a vision. Then he asked,
> "What do you see, Jeremiah?"
> I answered, "A branch of almonds that ripen early."
> "That's right," the LORD replied, "and I always rise early* to keep a promise."

A note of explanation reads:

> 1.11, 12 **almonds . . . rise early**: *In Hebrew 'almonds that ripen early'*
> *sounds like 'always rise early.'*

Another example of a play on words occurs in Genesis 2.23, where the note points out that the Hebrew words for "man" and "woman" are similar:

> "Here is someone like me!
> She is part of my body,
> my own flesh and bones.
> She came from me, a man.
> So I will name her Woman!"

A Mini Dictionary for the Bible

Although the *CEV* uses understandable everyday English wherever possible, some readers may discover terms that are new to them. A number of these are technical terms (like "Pharisees") that cannot be put into modern English. As a help to readers a Mini Dictionary for the Bible is included in the back of most *CEV* Bibles, with entries listed both alphabetically and under twenty-one different categories:

- A Few Basics
- Scriptures, Manuscripts
- Languages
- People
- Prophets

- Twelve Tribes of Israel
- Christ's Twelve Apostles
- Groups of People, Cities, Nations
- Places
- Objects
- Festivals and Holy Days
- Sacrifice, Temple, Worship
- Customs
- God, Jesus, Angels
- Foreign Gods, Fortunetellers, Evil Spirits
- Plants, Animals, and Farming
- Society and Its Leaders
- Families, Relatives
- Events
- Dates
- The Hebrew Calendar

Since many people come to the Bible with no previous Bible-reading experience, the fourth entry under *A Few Basics* will prove beneficial:

> *Chapter and Verse Numbers* These numbers were not part of the original books, but were added hundreds of years later as a way to refer to specific parts of the books of Scripture. For example, Genesis 1.3 means "the book of Genesis, chapter 1, verse 3." Genesis 2.4, 5 means "the book of Genesis, chapter 2, verses 4 through 5." And Genesis 1–2 means, "the book of Genesis, chapters 1 through 2." A few books are so short that they were not divided into chapters, and so these books only have verse numbers. In the text of the CEV, sometimes verse numbers have been combined, for example, 3-4. One reason verse numbers might be combined is that contemporary English says things in a different order than ancient Greek and Hebrew, and so two or more verses are sometimes blended together in the CEV translation. And in lists, the verse numbers are sometimes combined into a single heading to avoid confusion. But all the meaning from the original Greek and Hebrew has been carefully included in the CEV text.

All Verse Numbers Accounted For!

Wherever possible the *CEV* tries to adhere to the verse numbering system applied to the Scriptures hundreds of years ago. But because the structure of contemporary English is often quite different from that of ancient Hebrew and Greek, it has sometimes been necessary to restructure a short passage so that the meaning comes through to the reader as clearly as possible. As a result it can be nearly impossible to determine where one verse left off and the next one began. When two or three verses are handled in this way as a larger sense unit, *CEV,* like other modern translations, indicates this by using hyphenated verse markers to make clear the range of verses included. For example, Jude 24-25 indicates that the sentences which follow include the entire context of verses 24 through 25, though not necessarily in that order. This technique is especially useful for lists and genealogies as, for example, in Ezra 2.3-20 and Matthew 1.12-16.

There are also a few places in the Bible, most notably in the New Testament, where certain verses are not found in the oldest and best manuscripts available. Many translations resolve this difficulty simply by dropping the verse numbers of those verses missing from the text, but that can be confusing or alarming for readers. However, in the *CEV all* verse numbers are included, and the textual notes provide explanation. For example, in one traditional translation of Mark chapter 9, verse numbers 44 and 46 are omitted from the text and consigned to the footnotes. Verse 43 is accompanied by a note "Some manuscripts add verse 44," followed by the wording for that verse which lacks significant support in the ancient manuscripts. Although all the words are there on the page, when this happens the text itself still looks odd because of the missing numbers.

To avoid this kind of confusion, the *CEV* combines verse numbers with a hyphen and includes a note at the end of the combined verses. The note after [43-44] reads:

> **9.43-44 never go out:** *Some manuscripts add, "The worms there never die, and the fire never stops burning."*

An Occasional Asterisk (*)

An occasional asterisk (*) can be found in poetic passages. These indicate a slightly restructured passage where the usual, hyphenated verse numbering system has been suspended for the verses marked. An example is Job 3, where verses 18, 19 have been joined in translation. The original draft looked as follows:

[18-19]Everyone is there —
> where captives and slaves
> are free at last.

The published text appears with the asterisk, indicating combined verses:

*[18]Everyone is there —
> [19] where captives and slaves
> are free at last.

Bible translating is more than simply trying to find a modern-language equivalent for an ancient-language word. It involves careful consideration of how the intended readers will perceive and understand every aspect of the text, as explained elsewhere in this book. The many notes, introductions, and helps the translators have provided for the reader are the result of their effort to make clear the wide range of information that the earliest generations of Christians would most likely have understood automatically or taken for granted.

8
CONCLUSION:
A NEW APPROACH TO BIBLE TRANSLATION

So What? What's New?

As the previous chapters have explained, the *Contemporary English Version* of the Bible is unique among English translations because of its emphasis upon *hearing* and *understanding* a *spoken* text. Traditional translations consider primarily the needs of the *reader,* and often one who is familiar with biblical language and has grown accustomed to the numerous awkward constructions so frequently found in such translations. The *CEV* considers both the needs of the *reader* and those of the *hearer,* who may not be familiar with traditional biblical language and whose primary contact with the text comes through *hearing* it read aloud. In other words, the *CEV* puts into practice the words of the apostle Paul that "no one can have faith without *hearing* the message about Christ."

Several observations support this need for an emphasis upon the *hearing* of a text:

(1) More people hear the Bible read than read it for themselves.

(2) Our society is fast approaching a post-literate age.

(3) New readers tend to "sound out" a written text.

(4) Experienced readers often read poetry and lyrical prose aloud.

(5) Hearing reinforces comprehension.

(6) Hearing assists the process of memorization.

(7) Any text that expresses its message in a manner that is easy
for the ear to follow can be clearly rendered into print,
but the reverse is not always true.

The *Contemporary English Version*, like all other translations of the Bible, has as its primary concern *faithfulness* to the *meaning* of the biblical text. And so, it was translated directly from the original languages of the Scriptures. But the *CEV* goes the "second mile" in creating a text that can be read aloud without stumbling, heard without misunderstanding, and listened to with appreciation and enjoyment because the language is natural and the style is lucid and lyrical. This chapter serves as a summary of the various kinds of innovative techniques the *CEV* translators used to provide a text that is fresh and engaging.

Mute Punctuation Marks

While punctuation marks are a standard and expected part of our written language, they are often ignored by people when reading the Bible aloud. This results in a biblical text that can be seen, but not heard with comprehension. The *CEV* has consistently and carefully attempted to create a text that does not depend upon eye contact with punctuation marks for comprehension. The basic rule here is that punctuation marks are *silent* and should not be counted upon to convey the proper meaning in the *hearing* of a text.

For example, even the inclusion of a simple word like "And" at the beginning of a sentence can make a significant difference. Genesis 7.15,16 of the *CEV* reads, "Noah took a male and a female of every living creature with him, just as God had told him to do. *And* when they were all in the boat, God closed the door."

"And" at the beginning of the second sentence assists both the person who reads the text aloud and those who must depend upon hearing it read. Like all other punctuation marks, the period after "to do" is silent, and so the text without "And" could possibly be heard as, " ... just as God had told him to do when they were all in the boat ..." However, as the text now stands, the oral reader must pause briefly for a breath before "And," which will signal the hearer that a new sentence has begun.

Traditional translations — since they depend solely upon *eye* contact with a written text — do not concern themselves as much with the silence of punctuation, as may be seen from a few examples from Psalms.

The pair of rhetorical questions in Psalm 89.47 ("Why did you create us? For nothing?") may be heard as a single statement, "Why did you create us for nothing?" In the *CEV*, possible confusion is avoided by recasting them as a single question, "Why did you empty our lives of all meaning?"

"How great is your goodness" (Psalm 31.19), "how lovely is your temple" (Psalm 84.1), and "How deep are your thoughts" (Psalm 92.5) will probably be heard as questions instead of exclamations, because "how" followed by an adjective generally indicates a question. In the *CEV* these verses are restructured to avoid such complications for the hearer: "You are wonderful" (Psalm 31.19), "your temple is so lovely" (Psalm 84.1), and "your thoughts are too deep" (Psalm 92.5).

Problems with Pronouns

The translators of the *CEV* exercised caution in order to avoid pronouns that mislead the reader by pointing back to the wrong person or object.

One traditional translation of Hebrews 11.4, can easily mislead the reader. It says,

> By faith Abel offered God a better sacrifice than Cain did. By faith he was commended as a righteous man, when *God spoke* well of his offerings. And by faith *he still speaks*, even though *he is dead.*

If the rules of English grammar are to be followed, "he is dead" must refer back to God.

In the *CEV* of this same passage, the participants are clearly identified:

> Because Abel had faith, he offered God a better sacrifice than Cain did. God was pleased with him and his gift, and even though *Abel is* now *dead, his* faith still speaks for *him.*

Another translation encounters a similar difficulty in Luke 23.40, where God receives the same sentence as the thief on the cross: "Don't you fear *God?* You received the same sentence *he* did." Actually, the reference is to Jesus, who is mentioned earlier in the passage, but the *hearer* won't easily reach that conclusion. Note also "Their *words* are wicked lies; *they* are no longer wise or good" (Psalm 36.3), where *they* is supposed to refer back to the people who speak evil lies, rather than to the wicked lies themselves. Here are the same verses in *CEV:*

Luke 23.40

Don't you fear *God?* Aren't you getting the same punishment as *this man?*

Psalm 36.3

They tell deceitful lies,
and they don't have the sense
to live right.

From time to time, any translation could possibly fail to make a pronoun's reference clear, but the *CEV* was read aloud many times and listened to with care on each occasion, with the intent of minimizing the number of possible obstacles for those who must depend upon hearing the text read aloud.

Sentences that Flow

When someone is listening to a text, the order in which the information is given becomes an important factor in comprehension. Compare the two translations of Luke 11.38 and 17.20. The translation of Luke 11.38 in column **A** will be difficult to understand because of the separation between the subject ("Pharisee") and the verb ("was surprised"), while Luke 17.20 will be difficult because the hearer must retain in mind "having been asked by the Pharisees when the kingdom of God would come" before finally connecting "Once" with "Jesus." The *CEV* (column **B**) is easier because the information flow reflects natural, everyday spoken English:

Luke 11.38

A	**B**
But the Pharisee, noticing that Jesus did not first wash before the meal, was surprised.	The Pharisee was surprised that he did not wash his hands before eating.

Luke 17.20

Once, having been asked when the kingdom of God would come, Jesus replied, ...	Some Pharisees asked Jesus when God's kingdom would come. He answered, ...

Using a pronoun before mentioning the noun to which it refers may cause confusion and stumbling when reading aloud. For example, in Matthew 27.63 "we remember that while *he* was alive *that deceiver* said" can be taken as a reference to *two* separate individuals, simply because "he" comes before "that deceiver." However, in context, the reference is to *one* individual, which becomes immediately clear when the flow of information is natural: "we remember what *that liar* said while *he* was still alive" (*CEV*).

Paragraph Structure

Related to the matter of information flow is that of paragraph structure. If paragraphs are too complex, involving a series of flashbacks, parenthetical statements, quotations within quotations, or ellipses, the hearer will become discouraged and miss out on the intended meaning along the way. Compare the comprehension level of *CEV* (column **B**) with a traditional translation of Mark 11.31-33 (column **A**), when each is read aloud:

A	**B**
They started to argue among themselves: "What shall we say? If we answer, 'From God,' he will say, 'Why, then, did you not believe John?' But if we say, 'From human	They thought it over and said to each other, "We can't say that God gave John this right. Jesus will ask us why we didn't believe John. On the other hand, these people think that

A	B
beings . . .'" (They were afraid of the people, because everyone was convinced that John had been a prophet.) So their answer to Jesus was, "We don't know."	John was a prophet. So we can't say that it was merely some human who gave John the right to baptize." They were afraid of the crowd and told Jesus, "We don't know."

Syllable Accent

In the preparation of the *CEV*, attention was given to such details as the number of consecutively unaccented syllables. This is because a series of more than three unaccented syllables makes a text difficult to read aloud. Note, for example, how hard it is to read aloud the following two sentences aloud: "You yourselves admit, then, that you agree with what your ancestors did" (Luke 11.48) and "for it was better with me then than now" (Hosea 2.7). Both suffer from potential tongue twisters ("admit, then, that" and "then than"). But the first is doubly difficult because it consists of a lengthy series of unaccented syllables that do not permit the reader to pause for a breath. In the *CEV* every attempt has been made to avoid these and similar constructions that could possibly prove problematic for oral reading.

Unwanted Rhythm and Rhymes

In translating the Scriptures, great care should be taken never to produce a text that sounds jingly, especially if the rhyme or rhythmic pattern could possibly convey a message other than the one intended by the text itself: "The *cook took* up the *whole* haunch" (1 Samuel 9.24 = Dr. Seuss, *Hop on Pop*, "Hop pop, we hop on pop" and "Night fight, we fight all night."); "Simon, Simon! Listen! Satan" (Luke 22.31 = "Reuben, Reuben, I've been thinking"); "The kings of pagans have power over their people"; "a people who will produce the proper fruits" (Luke 22.25; Matthew 21.43 = Peter Piper).

Less disruptive, but of concern are (a) tongue twisters ("sowed weeds among the wheat and went away" and "among them were some women who were weeping and wailing") and (b) unintended rhymes ("After sending the people *away,* he went up on a hill to *pray*" and "who make themselves look *right* in other people's *sight*").

Misdirection Markers

In American football a "misdirection play" takes place when the team with the ball convinces the defense that the ball is being moved toward one side of the field, when it is actually being moved toward the opposite side. The purpose, of course, is to throw the defensive team off balance. Misdirection occurs also in translation, though unlike football, it is accidental and not deliberate. In translation there are numerous "odds and ends" that can throw the hearer of a text off balance, and it may easily happen when the hearer's expectations are contradicted. A prime example is the use of "for" as a conjunction, especially when it appears almost side-by-side with "for" as a preposition. In fact, "for" as a conjunction can almost always be replaced by "because" to make a clear, unambiguous statement.

Apart from the purely linguistic concerns, an even more urgent case against the use of "for" in this capacity is the misdirection it tends to give to the hearer, as in Revelation 18.2, 3 of one translation: "She has become a home *for* demons and a haunt *for* every evil spirit, a haunt *for* every unclean and detestable bird. *For* all the nations have drunk ..." The hearer could instinctively interpret "for all the nations" as a prepositional phrase parallel with the three that immediately precede it. Once this expectation is contradicted, the hearer may become frustrated and possibly lose interest in the rest of the Scripture reading.

Of some minor concern is the realization that in certain contexts "for" may be disguised as "four" as in "for wicked and deceitful men have opened their mouths against me" (Psalm 109.2).

"You who" (sounds like "yoo hoo") can also misdirect the hearer's attention and sometimes stir up a giggle, as in the following excerpt from Psalm 80.1:

> Hear us, O Shepherd of Israel,
>   *you who* lead Joseph like a flock;
>
> *you who* sit enthroned between the cherubim ...

Easy To Read, Pleasant To Hear, Easy To Pronounce

As someone has remarked, "A purchase of the *CEV* is a *sound* investment, because the translators have produced a text that is easy to read, pleasant to hear, and easy to pronounce." *Accuracy* is always the primary concern for translators — but beauty, clarity, and dignity should also be of concern, especially if there is any intention of using it for public worship. Psalm 19.1-4a of the *CEV* reflects such care in each of these aspects.

Observe how the majesty of the original is maintained by the choice of words, the mixture of rhythmic patterns, and even the sequence of consonants and vowels:

> The heavens keep telling
>   the wonders of God,
> and the skies declare
>   what he has done.
> Each day informs
>   the following day;
> each night announces
>   to the next.
> They don't speak a word,
> and there is never
>   the sound of a voice.
> Yet their message reaches
>   all the earth,
> and it travels
>   around the world.

In the translation of the Scriptures, a lyrical effect is just as important in prose as it is in poetry, especially when you consider that the majority of the biblical text is written in prose. Read the three following translations of Matthew 19.12 and judge which comes the closest to being lucid and lyrical:

A	**B**	**C**
For there are eunuchs who have been so from birth, and there are eunuchs who have been made eunuchs by others, and there are eunuchs who have made themselves eunuchs for the sake of the kingdom of heaven.	For there are different reasons why men cannot marry: some, because they were born that way; others, because men made them that way; and others do not marry for the sake of the Kingdom of heaven.	Some people are unable to marry because of birth defects or because of what someone has done to their bodies. Others stay single in order to serve God better.

The use of "eunuch" (literally, a castrated male) five times in one verse certainly makes **A** less than lucid or lyrical. In **B** the colon after "marry" cannot be heard, which means that "some" could be heard as the object of "marry" rather than as referring back to "men." Moreover, "because they were born that way" suggests that some men were born married.

Not only is the translation in column **C** (*CEV*) gender generic ("some people"; see chapter 6, p. 56 ff.), but a close reading will reveal that the same features of rhythm and sound are found here as in the passage from Psalm 19: "Some people are unable to marry" has a pleasing rhythm, as well as an "internal rhyme" ("people are unable"). The phrases "because of birth defects" and "because of what someone has done to their bodies" are balanced constructions that combine enjoyable stress patterns with pleasant consonant and vowel sounds. And finally, "in order to serve God better" both clarifies what is meant by "for the sake of the kingdom of heaven" and automatically slows down the oral reading of the text by requiring that "serve" and "God" and "better" each receive an accent.

If "faith comes by hearing", as the apostle Paul says, translators must give top priority to analyzing precisely *how* the text will be *heard* when read aloud. Nothing speaks more clearly to this issue than the Preface of the *Contemporary English Version:*

> Languages are spoken before they are written. And far more communication is done through th poken word than through the written word. In fac , nore people *hear* the Bible read than read it for ʟnemselves. Traditional translations of the Bible count on the *reader's* ability to understand a *written* text. But the *Contemporary English Version* differs from all other English Bibles — past and present — in that it takes into consideration the needs of the *hearer,* as well as those of the reader, who may not be familiar with traditional biblical language.

> The *Contemporary English Version*͵has been described as a "user- friendly" and a "mission-driven" translation that can be *read aloud* without stumbling, *heard* without misunderstanding, and *listened to* with enjoyment and appreciation, because the language is contemporary and the style is lucid and lyrical.

> The *Contemporary English Version* invites you to *read,* to *hear,* to *understand* and to *share*
> > *the Word of God now*
> > *as never before!*

Appendix A
THE MAKING OF THE CEV

Process and Personnel

The drafting, reviewing, editing, revising and refining the text of the *Contemporary English Version* has been a worldwide process extending over a period of slightly more than ten years. It has involved a wide variety of persons beyond the core team of ABS translators and the consultant experts who have worked closely with the team. The creative process has also involved scholar consultants and reviewers representing a wide range of church traditions and with expertise in such areas as Old Testament, New Testament, Hebrew language, Greek language, English language, linguistics, and poetry. In all, this process involved more than a hundred people in the various stages of the text creation and review process. And it is this process, carried out in constant prayer for the guidance of the Spirit of God, that guarantees the accuracy, integrity and trustworthiness of the *CEV* Bible.

Creative Core

At the core of the *CEV* development process has been the team of translators assembled by the American Bible Society specifically for that purpose. This creative core, a team of three translators and an editorial associate, has been responsible for producing an accurate translation in a style appropriate for the designated audience. Dr. Barclay M. Newman (Ph.D., Southern Baptist Theological Seminary, a biblical scholar with several decades of experience as a United Bible Societies Translation Consultant in the Asia Pacific region) planned and organized the *CEV* project with the aid of Dr. Eugene A. Nida, a Special Consultant to the ABS. Beginning in 1984, Newman carried out research in preparation for this project, initiated the translation work that ensued, and throughout the next decade guided the overall project to its publication targets, with the New Testament appearing in 1991, the Psalms and Proverbs in 1992, and the Bible in 1995 (an edition of the Bible with the Deuterocanonicals/Apocrypha is scheduled for publication in 1997). The rest of the *CEV* team has consisted of Dr. Donald A. Johns (Ph.D., St. Louis University), Dr. Steven W. Berneking (Ph.D., Union Theological Seminary), and Mrs. M. Jean Newman, who has served as editorial associate throughout the project, handling a variety of the editorial and stylistic responsibilities as part of the CEV team.

Scholarly Scrutiny

Every attempt was made to produce a text that is faithful to the *meaning* of the original. In order to assure the *accuracy* of the *Contemporary English Version,* the Old Testament was translated directly from the Hebrew and Aramaic texts published by the United Bible Societies (*Biblia Hebraica Stuttgartensia,* fourth edition corrected). And the New Testament was translated directly from the Greek text published by the United Bible Societies (third edition corrected, compared with the fourth revised edition as it came into existence during the time the *CEV* New Testament was being developed).

If translation is the faithful and systematic communication of meaning from one language to another, then it becomes absolutely necessary to have a diverse array of scholars assigned to check the translation for faithfulness and accuracy. As the drafts of the individual books of the *CEV* emerged from the core team, they were checked for faithfulness to the Hebrew, Aramaic and Greek texts, as well as for style, accuracy and effectiveness as a translation, by an international roster of biblical scholars — both Christian and Jewish — as well as linguists, English language experts, specialists in poetry and style, and denominational reviewers. This process involved the worldwide circulation of draft texts for review and critique, and the subsequent editing and refinement of drafts in the light of the responses received. At times this required extended discussion of issues that had been raised among the members of the ABS Board's Translations Subcommittee, or lengthy telephone conversations and correspondence with reviewers, but no text was recommended for publication until every concern that was raised had been discussed and resolved.

The process involved sending out copies of the *CEV* drafts in their earliest stages for review and critique by all the biblical scholars, theologians, educators and specialists on the ABS review list, representing a wide variety of church traditions. At its broadest scope this list included representatives of all the Bible Societies around the world with sizeable English-speaking populations and more than forty UBS Translation Consultants worldwide, whose collective experience and expertise in a variety of scholarly disciplines is most significant. Final approval of texts, book by book, was given by the ABS Board of Trustees, upon the recommendation of the Program Committee and its Translations Subcommittee.

It must be acknowledged that the *CEV's* development over the past decade is a clear example of the truth that translation work is never carried out in a vacuum. The regular input and critiquing of the drafts by various representatives of different church traditions was both substantive and valuable to the development and final shaping of the translation. At all the review and check-points along the way it was most important to have received reactions from the reviewers who could signal how the *CEV* would work (or work better) from the viewpoints of various traditions. The *CEV* benefitted immeasurably from the collective vision and sensitivity of reviewers at this level. From the outset Dr. Eugene A. Nida served as a special consultant to the team. Ms. Evelyn R. Tower served as a special consultant on poetry and style. Dr. Erroll F. Rhodes provided close exegetical review for the books of both Old and New Testaments, as did the late Dr. Dewey M. Beegle, Old Testament specialist, and Dr. Howard Clark Kee, New Testament specialist. And the members of the ABS Board's Translations Subcommittee — its scholarly review committee — also made a notable commitment to immersing themselves in the review process with dedicated scholarship.

While it would be easy to give credit only to the translators who prepared the original drafts of the *CEV* and who are the creative core of the translation effort, it is important to remember that the process truly represents the cumulative effort of all those involved at every level of the process. And for that reason the ABS is deeply grateful to God, and to all who participated in the process.

Appendix B
SAMPLE *CEV* TEXTS

This appendix provides samples of Scripture passages as they appear in typical, double-column format Bibles. Each passage is printed with its section heading. The passages were chosen to showcase different important aspects of the *Contemporary English Version* text.

CLEAR AND LIVELY NARRATIVE

GENESIS 32.22-32

Jacob's Name Is Changed to Israel

22-23Jacob got up in the middle of the night and took his wives, his eleven children, and everything he owned across to the other side of the Jabbok River for safety. 24Afterwards, Jacob went back and spent the rest of the night alone.

A man came and fought with Jacob until just before daybreak. 25When the man saw that he could not win, he struck Jacob on the hip and threw it out of joint. 26They kept on wrestling until the man said, "Let go of me! It's almost daylight."

"You can't go until you bless me," Jacob replied.

27Then the man asked, "What is your name?"

"Jacob," he answered.

28The man said, "Your name will no longer be Jacob. You have wrestled with God and with men, and you have won. That's why your name will be Israel."a

29Jacob said, "Now tell me your name."

"Don't you know who I am?" he asked. And he blessed Jacob.

30Jacob said, "I have seen God face to face, and I am still alive." So he named the place Peniel.b 31The sun was coming up as Jacob was leaving Peniel. He was limping because he had been struck on the hip, 32and the muscle on his hip joint had been injured. That's why even today the people of Israel don't eat the hip muscle of any animal.

___

a**Israel:** *In Hebrew one meaning of "Israel" is "a man who wrestles with God."* b**Peniel:** *In Hebrew "Peniel" means "face of God."*

MAKING LISTS AND GENEALOGIES EASY TO FOLLOW

1 CHRONICLES 3.1-9

The Descendants of King David

3 [1-4]King David ruled from Hebron for seven years and six months, and during that time he had six sons, who were born in the following order: Amnon, Daniel, Absalom, Adonijah, Shephatiah, and Ithream. Ahinoam from Jezreel was the mother of Amnon; Abigail from Carmel was the mother of Daniel; Maacah daughter of King Talmai of Geshur was the mother of Absalom; Haggith was the mother of Adonijah; Abital was the mother of Shephatiah; and Eglah was the mother of Ithream.

David then ruled from Jerusalem for thirty-three years, [5]and during that time, he had thirteen more sons. His wife Bathsheba[a] daughter of Ammiel gave birth to Shimea, Shobab, Nathan, and Solomon. [6-8]David's other sons included Ibhar, Elishua,[b] Eliphelet, Nogah, Nepheg, Japhia, Elishama, Eliada, and Eliphelet. [9]David's other wives[c] also gave birth to sons. Tamar was his daughter.

_____

[a]**Bathsheba:** *Two ancient translations (see also 2 Samuel 11); Hebrew "Bathshua."* [b]**Elishua:** *Some Hebrew manuscripts and some manuscripts of one ancient translation (see also 2 Samuel 5.14,15); most Hebrew manuscripts "Elishama."* [c]**other wives:** *This translates a Hebrew word for women who were legally bound to a man, but without the full privileges of a wife.*

MATTHEW 1.1-17

The Ancestors of Jesus

(Luke 3.23–38)

1 Jesus Christ came from the family of King David and also from the family of Abraham. And this is a list of his ancestors. [2-6a]From Abraham to King David, his ancestors were:

Abraham, Isaac, Jacob, Judah and his brothers (Judah's sons were Perez and Zerah, and their mother was Tamar), Hezron;

Ram, Amminadab, Nahshon, Salmon, Boaz (his mother was Rahab), Obed (his mother was Ruth), Jesse, and King David.

[6b-11]From David to the time of the exile in Babylonia, the ancestors of Jesus were:

David, Solomon (his mother had been Uriah's wife), Rehoboam, Abijah, Asa, Jehoshaphat, Jehoram;

Uzziah, Jotham, Ahaz, Hezekiah, Manasseh, Amon, Josiah, and Jehoiachin and his brothers.

[12-16]From the exile to the birth of Jesus, his ancestors were:

Jehoiachin, Shealtiel, Zerubbabel, Abiud, Eliakim, Azor, Zadok, Achim;

Eliud, Eleazar, Matthan, Jacob, and Joseph, the husband of Mary, the mother of Jesus, who is called the Messiah.

[17]There were fourteen generations from Abraham to David. There were also fourteen from David to the exile in Babylonia and fourteen more to the birth of the Messiah.

USING RESTRUCTURING TO MAKE DIFFICULT PASSAGES CLEAR

JOHN 1.1-18

The Word of Life

1 In the beginning was the one
who is called the Word.
The Word was with God
and was truly God.

² From the very beginning
the Word was with God.

˙ And with this Word,
God created all things.
Nothing was made
without the Word.
Everything that was created
⁴ received its life from him,
and his life gave light
to everyone.

⁵ The light keeps shining
in the dark,
and darkness has never
put it out.ª

⁶ God sent a man named John,
⁷ who came to tell
about the light
and to lead all people
to have faith.

⁸ John wasn't that light.
He came only to tell
about the light.

⁹ The true light that shines
on everyone
was coming into the world.

¹⁰ The Word was in the world,
but no one knew him,
though God had made the world
with his Word.

¹¹ He came into his own world,
but his own nation
did not welcome him.

¹² Yet some people accepted him
and put their faith in him.
So he gave them the right
to be the children of God.

¹³ They were not God's children
by nature or because
of any human desires.
God himself was the one
who made them his children.

¹⁴ The Word became
a human being
and lived here with us.
We saw his true glory,
the glory of the only Son
of the Father.
From him all the kindness
and all the truth of God
have come down to us.

¹⁵John spoke about him and shouted, "This is the one I told you would come! He is greater than I am, because he was alive before I was born."

¹⁶Because of all that the Son is, we have been given one blessing after another.ᵇ ¹⁷The Law was given by Moses, but Jesus Christ brought us undeserved kindness and truth. ¹⁸ No one has ever seen God. The only Son, who is truly God and is closest to the Father, has shown us what God is like.

ªput it out: *Or "understood it."* ᵇone blessing after another: *Or "one blessing in place of another."*

Romans 5.1-11

What It Means To Be Acceptable to God

5 By faith we have been made acceptable to God. And now, because of our Lord Jesus Christ, we live at peace[a] with God. [2]Christ has also introduced us[b] to God's undeserved kindness on which we take our stand. So we are happy, as we look forward to sharing in the glory of God. [3]But that's not all! We gladly suffer,[c] because we know that suffering helps us to endure. [4]And endurance builds character, which gives us a hope [5]that will never disappoint us. All of this happens because God has given us the Holy Spirit, who fills our hearts with his love.

[6]Christ died for us at a time when we were helpless and sinful. [7]No one is really willing to die for an honest person, though someone might be willing to die for a truly good person. [8]But God showed how much he loved us by having Christ die for us, even though we were sinful.

[9] But there is more! Now that God has accepted us because Christ sacrificed his life's blood, we will also be kept safe from God's anger. [10] Even when we were God's enemies, he made peace with us, because his Son died for us. Yet something even greater than friendship is ours. Now that we are at peace with God, we will be saved by his Son's life. [11] And in addition to everything else, we are happy because God sent our Lord Jesus Christ to make peace with us.

----

[a]**we live at peace:** *Some manuscripts have "let us live at peace." * [b]**introduced us:** *Some manuscripts add "by faith." * [c]**We gladly suffer:** *Or "Let us gladly suffer."*

MAKING QUOTATIONS EASY TO FOLLOW

Song of Songs 2.8-15

Winter Is Past

She Speaks:
[8]　I hear the voice
　　　of the one I love,
　　as he comes leaping
　　over mountains and hills
[9]　　like a deer or a gazelle.
　　Now he stands outside our wall,
　　looking through the window
[10]　　and speaking to me.

He Speaks:
　　My darling, I love you!
　　　Let's go away together.
[11]　Winter is past,
　　　the rain has stopped;
[12]　flowers cover the earth,
　　　it's time to sing.[a]

　　The cooing of doves
　　　is heard in our land.
[13]　Fig trees are bearing fruit,
　　　while blossoms on grapevines
　　　　fill the air with perfume.
　　My darling, I love you!
　　　Let's go away together.
[14]　You are my dove
　　　hiding among the rocks
　　　　on the side of a cliff.
　　Let me see how lovely you are!
　　Let me hear the sound
　　　of your melodious voice.
[15]　Our vineyards are in blossom;
　　　we must catch the little foxes
　　　　that destroy the vineyards.[b]

----

[a]**sing:** *Or "trim the vines." * [b]**vineyards:** *One possible meaning for the difficult Hebrew text of verse 15.*

MATTHEW 5.1-16

The Sermon on the Mount

5 When Jesus saw the crowds, he went up on the side of a mountain and sat down.[a]

Blessings
(Luke 6.20–23)

Jesus' disciples gathered around him, [2]and he taught them:

[3]   God blesses those people
     who depend only on him.
   They belong to the kingdom
     of heaven![b]

[4]   God blesses those people
   who grieve.
     They will find comfort!

[5]   God blesses those people
   who are humble.
   The earth will belong
     to them!

[6]   God blesses those people
   who want to obey him[c]
     more than to eat or drink.
   They will be given
     what they want!

[7]   God blesses those people
   who are merciful.
   They will be treated
     with mercy!

[8]   God blesses those people
   whose hearts are pure.
     They will see him!

[9]   God blesses those people
   who make peace.
   They will be called
     his children!

[10]   God blesses those people
who are treated badly
     for doing right.
They belong to the kingdom
     of heaven.[d]

[11]God will bless you when people insult you, mistreat you, and tell all kinds of evil lies about you because of me. [12]Be happy and excited! You will have a great reward in heaven. People did these same things to the prophets who lived long ago.

Salt and Light
(Mark 9.50; Luke 14.34,35)

[13]You are like salt for everyone on earth. But if salt no longer tastes like salt, how can it make food salty? All it is good for is to be thrown out and walked on.

[14]You are like light for the whole world. A city built on top of a hill cannot be hidden, [15]and no one would light a lamp and put it under a clay pot. A lamp is placed on a lampstand, where it can give light to everyone in the house. [16]Make your light shine, so that others will see the good that you do and will praise your Father in heaven.

---

[a]**sat down:** *Teachers in the ancient world, including Jewish teachers, usually sat down when they taught.* [b]**They belong to the kingdom of heaven:** *Or "The kingdom of heaven belongs to them."* [c]**who want to obey him:** *Or "who want to do right" or "who want everyone to be treated right."* [d]**They belong to the kingdom of heaven:** *See the note at 5.3.*

Luke 4.14-21

Jesus Begins His Work
(Matthew 4.12–17; Mark 1.14,15)

[14]Jesus returned to Galilee with the power of the Spirit. News about him spread everywhere. [15]He taught in the Jewish meeting places, and everyone praised him.

The People of Nazareth Turn against Jesus
(Matthew 13.53-58; Mark 6.1-6)

[16]Jesus went back to Nazareth, where he had been brought up, and as usual he went to the meeting place on the Sabbath. When he stood up to read from the Scriptures, [17]he was given the book of Isaiah the prophet. He opened it and read,

[18] "The Lord's Spirit
    has come to me,
because he has chosen me
to tell the good news
    to the poor.
The Lord has sent me
to announce freedom
    for prisoners,
to give sight to the blind,
to free everyone
    who suffers,
[19]   and to say, 'This is the year
        the Lord has chosen.'"

[20]Jesus closed the book, then handed it back to the man in charge and sat down. Everyone in the meeting place looked straight at Jesus. [21]Then Jesus said to them, "What you have just heard me read has come true today."

BEAUTIFUL POETRY THAT'S EASY TO FOLLOW

Genesis 1.1–2.3

The Story of Creation

1 In the beginning God
    created the heavens
        and the earth.[a]
[2] The earth was barren,
        with no form of life;[b]
    it was under a roaring ocean
        covered with darkness.
    But the Spirit of God[c]
        was moving over the water.

The First Day

[3]God said, "I command light to shine!" And light started shining. [4]God looked at the light and saw that it was good. He separated light from darkness [5]and named the light "Day" and the darkness "Night." Evening came and then morning—that was the first day.[d]

The Second Day

[6]God said, "I command a dome to separate the water above it from the water below it." [7]And that's what happened. God made the dome [8]and named it "Sky." Evening came and then morning—that was the second day.

The Third Day

[9]God said, "I command the water under the sky to come together in one place, so there will be dry ground." And that's what happened. [10]God named the dry ground "Land," and he named the water "Ocean." God looked at what he had done and saw that it was good.

[11]God said, "I command the earth to produce all kinds of plants, including fruit trees and grain." And that's what happened. [12]The earth produced all kinds of vegetation. God looked at what he had done, and it was good. [13]Evening came and then morning—that was the third day.

The Fourth Day

¹⁴God said, "I command lights to appear in the sky and to separate day from night and to show the time for seasons, special days, and years. ¹⁵I command them to shine on the earth." And that's what happened. ¹⁶God made two powerful lights, the brighter one to rule the day and the other *ᵉ* to rule the night. He also made the stars. ¹⁷Then God put these lights in the sky to shine on the earth, ¹⁸to rule day and night, and to separate light from darkness. God looked at what he had done, and it was good. ¹⁹Evening came and then morning—that was the fourth day.

The Fifth Day

²⁰God said, "I command the ocean to be full of living creatures, and I command birds to fly above the earth." ²¹So God made the giant sea monsters and all the living creatures that swim in the ocean. He also made every kind of bird. God looked at what he had done, and it was good. ²²Then he gave the living creatures his blessing—he told the ocean creatures to live everywhere in the ocean and the birds to live everywhere on earth. ²³Evening came and then morning—that was the fifth day.

The Sixth Day

²⁴God said, "I command the earth to give life to all kinds of tame animals, wild animals, and reptiles." And that's what happened. ²⁵God made every one of them. Then he looked at what he had done, and it was good.

²⁶God said, "Now we will make humans, and they will be like us. We will let them rule the fish, the birds, and all other living creatures."

²⁷So God created humans to be like himself; he made men and women. ²⁸God gave them his blessing and said:

Have a lot of children! Fill the earth with people and bring it under your control. Rule over the fish in the ocean, the birds in the sky, and every animal on the earth.

²⁹I have provided all kinds of fruit and grain for you to eat. ³⁰And I have given the green plants as food for everything else that breathes. These will be food for animals, both wild and tame, and for birds.

³¹God looked at what he had done. All of it was very good! Evening came and then morning—that was the sixth day.

2 So the heavens and the earth and everything else were created.

The Seventh Day

²By the seventh day God had finished his work, and so he rested. ³God blessed the seventh day and made it special because on that day he rested from his work.

ᵃ **the heavens and the earth:** *"The heavens and the earth" stood for the universe.* *ᵇ* **In ... life:** *Or "When God began to create the heavens and the earth, the earth was barren with no form of life."* *ᶜ* **the Spirit of God:** *Or "a mighty wind."* *ᵈ* **the first day:** *A day was measured from evening to evening.* *ᵉ* **the brighter ... the other:** *The sun and the moon. But they are not called by their names, because in Old Testament times some people worshiped the sun and the moon as though they were gods.*

GENESIS 25.19-26

The Birth of Esau and Jacob

[19]Isaac was the son of Abraham, [20]and he was forty years old when he married Rebekah, the daughter of Bethuel. She was also the sister of Laban, the Aramean from northern Syria.[a]

Almost twenty years later, [21]Rebekah still had no children. So Isaac asked the LORD to let her have a child, and the LORD answered his prayer.

[22]Before Rebekah gave birth, she knew she was going to have twins, because she could feel them inside her, fighting each other. She thought, "Why is this happening to me?" Finally, she asked the LORD why her twins were fighting, [23]and he told her:

"Your two sons will become
  two separate nations.[b]
The younger of the two
  will be stronger,
and the older son
  will be his servant."

[24]When Rebekah gave birth, [25]the first baby was covered with red hair, so he was named Esau.[c] [26]The second baby grabbed on to his brother's heel, so they named him Jacob.[d] Isaac was sixty years old when they were born.

_____

[a]**northern Syria:** *See the note at 24.10.* [b] **two separate nations:** *Or "two nations always in conflict."* [c]**Esau:** *In Hebrew "Esau" sounds like "hairy."* [d]**Jacob:** *In Hebrew "Jacob" sounds like "heel."*

PSALM 18

[For the music leader. A psalm by David, the LORD's servant. David sang this to the LORD after the LORD had rescued him from his enemies, but especially from Saul.]

David's Song of Thanks

1 I love you, LORD God,
     and you make me strong.
2 You are my mighty rock,[a]
     my fortress, my protector,
   the rock where I am safe,
   my shield, my powerful weapon,[b]
     and my place of shelter.

3 I praise you, LORD!
   I prayed, and you rescued me
     from my enemies.
4 Death had wrapped

its ropes around me,
and I was almost swallowed
  by its flooding waters.

5 Ropes from the world
   of the dead
       had coiled around me,
   and death had set a trap
       in my path.
6 I was in terrible trouble
       when I called out to you,
   but from your temple
   you heard me
       and answered my prayer.
7 The earth shook and shivered,
   and the mountains trembled
       down to their roots.
   You were angry
8   and breathed out smoke.
   Scorching heat and fiery flames
       spewed from your mouth

9 You opened the heavens
    like curtains,
and you came down
    with storm clouds
      under your feet.
10 You rode on the backs
    of flying creatures
and swooped down
    with the wind as wings.
11 Darkness was your robe;
thunderclouds filled the sky,
    hiding you from sight.
12 Hailstones and fiery coals
lit up the sky
    in front of you.

13 LORD Most High, your voice
    thundered from the heavens,
as hailstones and fiery coals
    poured down like rain.
14 You scattered your enemies
    with arrows of lightning.
15 You roared at the sea,
and its deepest channels
    could be seen.
You snorted,
and the earth shook
    to its foundations.

16 You reached down from heaven,
and you lifted me
    from deep in the ocean.
17 You rescued me from enemies,
who were hateful
    and too powerful for me.
18 On the day disaster struck,
they came and attacked,
    but you defended me.
19 When I was fenced in,
you freed and rescued me
    because you love me.

20 You are good to me, LORD,
    because I do right,
and you reward me
    because I am innocent.
21 I do what you want
    and never turn to do evil.
22 I keep your laws in mind
and never look away
    from your teachings.
23 I obey you completely
    and guard against sin.
24 You have been good to me
    because I do right;
you have rewarded me
for being innocent
    by your standards.

25 You are always loyal
    to your loyal people,
and you are faithful
    to the faithful.
26 With all who are sincere,
    you are sincere,
but you treat the unfaithful
    as their deeds deserve.
27 You rescue the humble,
but you put down all
    who are proud.

28 You, the LORD God,
keep my lamp burning
    and turn darkness to light.
29 You help me defeat armies
    and capture cities.

30 Your way is perfect, LORD,
    and your word is correct.
You are a shield for those
    who run to you for help.

³¹ You alone are God!
> Only you are a mighty rock.^c

³² You give me strength
> and guide me right.

³³ You make my feet run as fast
> as those of a deer,
and you help me stand
> on the mountains.

³⁴ You teach my hands to fight
and my arms to use
> a bow of bronze.

³⁵ You alone are my shield.
> Your right hand supports me,
and by coming to help me,
> you have made me famous.

³⁶ You clear the way for me,
> and now I won't stumble.

³⁷ I kept chasing my enemies,
until I caught them
> and destroyed them.

³⁸ I stuck my sword
> through my enemies,
and they were crushed
> under my feet.

³⁹ You helped me win victories,
and you forced my attackers
> to fall victim to me.

⁴⁰ You made my enemies run,
> and I killed them.

⁴¹ They cried out for help,
> but no one saved them;
they called out to you,
> but there was no answer.

⁴² I ground them to dust
> blown by the wind,
and I poured them out
> like mud in the streets.

⁴³ You rescued me
> from stubborn people,
and you made me the leader
of foreign nations,
> who are now my slaves.

⁴⁴ They obey and come crawling.

⁴⁵   They have lost all courage,
and from their fortresses,
> they come trembling.

⁴⁶ You are the living Lord!
> I will praise you.
You are a mighty rock.^c
I will honor you
> for keeping me safe.

⁴⁷ You took revenge for me,
and you put nations
> in my power.

⁴⁸ You protected me
> from violent enemies
and made me much greater
> than all of them.

⁴⁹ I will praise you, Lord,
and I will honor you
> among the nations.

⁵⁰ You give glorious victories
> to your chosen king.
Your faithful love for David
and for his descendants
> will never end.

---

^a**mighty rock:** *The Hebrew text has "rock," which is sometimes used in poetry to compare the Lord to a mountain where his people can run for protection from their enemies.* ^b**my powerful weapon:** *The Hebrew text has "the horn," which refers to the horn of a bull, one of the most powerful animals in ancient Palestine.* ^c**mighty rock:** *See the note at 18.2.*

Proverbs 3.1-10

Trust God

3 My child, remember
my teachings and instructions
and obey them completely.
² They will help you live
a long and prosperous life.
³ Let love and loyalty
always show like a necklace,
and write them in your mind.
⁴ God and people will like you
and consider you a success.

⁵ With all your heart
you must trust the LORD

and not your own judgment.
⁶ Always let him lead you,
and he will clear the road
for you to follow.
⁷ Don't ever think that you
are wise enough,
but respect the LORD
and stay away from evil.
⁸ This will make you healthy,
and you will feel strong.
⁹ Honor the LORD by giving him
your money and the first part
of all your crops.
¹⁰ Then you will have
more grain and grapes
than you will ever need.

Isaiah 11.1-9

Peace at Last

11 Like a branch that sprouts
from a stump,
someone from David's family^a
will someday be king.
² The Spirit of the LORD
will be with him
to give him understanding,
wisdom, and insight.
He will be powerful,
and he will know
and honor the LORD.
³ His greatest joy will be
to obey the LORD.

This king won't judge
by appearances
or listen to rumors.
⁴ The poor and the needy
will be treated with fairness
and with justice.

His word will be law
everywhere in the land,
and criminals
will be put to death.
⁵ Honesty and fairness
will be his royal robes.

⁶ Leopards will lie down
with young goats,
and wolves will rest
with lambs.
Calves and lions
will eat together
and be cared for
by little children.
⁷ Cows and bears will share
the same pasture;
their young will rest
side by side.
Lions and oxen
will both eat straw.

⁸ Little children will play
near snake holes.

They will stick their hands
into dens of poisonous snakes
and never be hurt.

⁹ Nothing harmful will take place
on the LORD's holy mountain.
Just as water fills the sea,

the land will be filled
with people who know
and honor the LORD.

_____

*ᵃ**David's family:** Hebrew "Jesse's family." Jesse was the father of King David.*

REVELATION 1.4-8

⁴ From John to the seven churches in Asia.ᵃ
I pray that you
will be blessed
with kindness and peace
from God, who is and was
and is coming.
May you receive
kindness and peace
from the seven spirits
before the throne of God.
⁵ May kindness and peace
be yours
from Jesus Christ,
the faithful witness.

Jesus was the first
to conquer death,
and he is the ruler
of all earthly kings.
Christ loves us,
and by his blood
he set us free

from our sins.
⁶ He lets us rule as kings
and serve God his Father
as priests.
To him be glory and power
forever and ever! Amen.
⁷ Look! He is coming
with the clouds.
Everyone will see him,
even the ones who stuck
a sword through him.
All people on earth
will weep because of him.
Yes, it will happen! Amen.
⁸The Lord God says, "I am Alpha and Omega,ᵇ the one who is and was and is coming. I am God All-Powerful!"

_____

*ᵃ**Asia:** The section 1.4–3.22 is in the form of a letter. Asia was in the eastern part of the Roman Empire and is present day Turkey. ᵇ**Alpha and Omega:** The first and last letters of the Greek alphabet, which sometimes mean "first" and "last."*

SOME FAVORITE AND FAMILIAR PASSAGES

EXODUS 20.1-17

The Ten Commandments

(Deuteronomy 5.1-21)

20 God said to the people of Israel:
²I am the LORD your God, the one who

brought you out of Egypt where you were slaves.
³Do not worship any god except me.
⁴Do not make idols that look like anything in the sky or on earth or in the ocean under the earth. ⁵Don't bow down and worship idols. I am the LORD your God, and I demand all your love. If you reject me, I will punish your families for

three or four generations. ⁶But if you love me and obey my laws, I will be kind to your families for thousands of generations.

⁷Do not misuse my name.ᵃ I am the LORD your God, and I will punish anyone who misuses my name.

⁸Remember that the Sabbath Day belongs to me. ⁹You have six days when you can do your work, ¹⁰but the seventh day of each week belongs to me, your God. No one is to work on that day — not you, your children, your slaves, your animals, or the foreigners who live in your towns. ¹¹In six days I made the sky, the earth, the oceans, and everything in them, but on the seventh day I rested. That's why I made the Sabbath a special day that belongs to me.

¹²Respect your father and your mother, and you will live a long time in the land I am giving you.

¹³Do not murder.

¹⁴Be faithful in marriage.

¹⁵Do not steal.

¹⁶Do not tell lies about others.

¹⁷Do not want anything that belongs to someone else. Don't want anyone's house, wife or husband, slaves, oxen, donkeys or anything else.

_____

ᵃ **misuse my name:** *Probably includes breaking promises, telling lies after swearing to tell the truth, using the LORD's name as a curse word or a magic formula, and trying to control the LORD by using his name.*

PSALM 23

[A psalm by David.]

The Good Shepherd

¹ You, LORD, are my shepherd.
  I will never be in need.
² You let me rest in fields
  of green grass.
 You lead me to streams
 of peaceful water,
³   and you refresh my life.

 You are true to your name,
 and you lead me
  along the right paths.
⁴ I may walk through valleys
 as dark as death,
  but I won't be afraid.

You are with me,
and your shepherd's rodᵃ
  makes me feel safe.

⁵ You treat me to a feast,
  while my enemies watch.
 You honor me as your guest,
 and you fill my cup
  until it overflows.
⁶ Your kindness and love
 will always be with me
  each day of my life,
 and I will live forever
  in your house, LORD.

_____

ᵃ **shepherd's rod:** *The Hebrew text mentions two objects carried by the shepherd: a club to defend against wild animals and a long pole to guide and control the sheep.*

Isaiah 7.10-17

A Son Named Immanuel

[10] Once again the LORD God spoke to King Ahaz. This time he said, [11]"Ask me for proof that my promise will come true. Ask for something to happen deep in the world of the dead or high in the heavens above."

[12]"No, LORD," Ahaz answered. "I won't test you!"

[13]Then I said:

Listen, every one of you in the royal family of David. You have already tried my patience. Now you are trying God's patience by refusing to ask for proof. [14]But the LORD will still give you proof. A virgin[a] is pregnant; she will have a son and will name him Immanuel.[b] [15-16]Even before the boy is old enough to know how to chose between right and wrong, he will eat yogurt and honey,[c] and the countries of the two kings you fear will be destroyed. [17]But the LORD will make more trouble for your people and your kingdom than any of you have known since Israel broke away from Judah. He will even bring the king of Assyria to attack you.

_____

[a]virgin: Or "young woman." In this context the difficult Hebrew word did not imply a virgin birth. However, in the Greek translation made about 200 B.C. and used by the early Christians, the word parthenos *had a double meaning. While the translator took it to mean "young woman," Matthew understood it to mean "virgin" and quoted the passage (Matthew 1.23) because it was the appropriate description of Mary, the mother of Jesus.* [b]Immanuel: *In Hebrew "Immanuel" means "God is with us."* [c]yogurt and honey: *This may refer either to expensive foods eaten in a time of plenty or to a limited diet eaten in times of a food shortage.*

Ecclesiastes 3.1-8

Everything Has Its Time

3 Everything on earth
　has its own time
　　and its own season.
[2] There is a time
　for birth and death,
　　planting and reaping,
[3] for killing and healing,
　　destroying and building,
[4] for crying and laughing,
　weeping and dancing,
[5] for throwing stones
　and gathering stones,
　　embracing and parting.
[6] There is a time
　for finding and losing,
　　keeping and giving,
[7] for tearing and sewing,
　　listening and speaking.
[8] There is also a time
　for love and hate,
　　for war and peace.

2 JOHN 4-11

Truth and Love

⁴I was very glad to learn that some of your children are obeying the truth, as the Father told us to do. ⁵Dear friend, I am not writing to tell you and your children to do something you have not done before. I am writing to tell you to love each other, which is the first thing you were told to do. ⁶Love means that we do what God tells us. And from the beginning, he told you to love him.

⁷Many liars have gone out into the world. These deceitful liars are saying that Jesus Christ did not have a truly human body. But they are liars and the enemies of Christ. ⁸So be sure not to lose what we[a] have worked for. If you do, you won't be given your full reward. ⁹Don't keep changing what you were taught about Christ, or else God will no longer be with you. But if you hold firmly to what you were taught, both the Father and the Son will be with you. ¹⁰If people won't agree to this teaching, don't welcome them into your home or even greet them. ¹¹Greeting them is the same as taking part in their evil deeds.

_____

[a]**we:** *Some manuscripts have "you."*

Appendix C

AMERICAN BIBLE SOCIETY

MISSION STATEMENT

The purpose of the American Bible Society is to provide the Holy Scriptures to every man, woman and child in a language and form each can readily understand, and at a price each can easily afford. This purpose, undertaken without doctrinal note or comment, and without profit, is a cause which all Christians and all churches are urged to support.